I0625317

ASK YOURSELF.

Ask Yourself.

Understand and Unlock Your Psychic Power for Personal & Planetary Healing

Pamela Irene Flowerday

Ask Yourself.
Understand and Unlock Your Psychic Power for Personal & Planetary Healing
Copyright © 2024 Rev. Pamela Irene Flowerday

All Rights Reserved. This book may not be reproduced, transmitted, or stored in whole or in part by any means, including graphic, electronic, or mechanical without the express written consent of the publisher except in the case of brief quotations embodied in critical articles and reviews.

ISBN: 979-8-218-41897-7

Cover art: Benjavisa Ruangvaree © 2023 istock. All rights reserved, used with permission.

Previously published by Outskirts Press, Inc., 2023
ISBN: 978-19772-5754-3

Printed in The United States of America

For my mother,
whose adventurous spiritual nature
encouraged my early metaphysical interests.

Acknowledgments

A heartfelt thanks to my best friend, Kimberley. Together, at the age of seven, we discovered "buried treasure" beneath a rock, officially launching my enthusiasm for magic and the power of play. Thanks for believing in my book and giving me that needed shove over the finish line. I acknowledge, with gratitude, the late Lewis Bostwick, founder of the Berkeley Psychic Institute, for creating the original clairvoyant training model that spawned so many exceptional psychic schools in the SF Bay Area. Thank you to all of my teachers at Psychic Horizons (San Francisco) and Aesclepion (Marin) for your dedication and patient guidance. I am indebted to Laura Hopper, Shirley Edwards, Judy Tergis, Bruce Van Horn, Tim Michaels, Paul Gifford, Michelle Comeau and Don Narin. Thanks to Ted Jalbert for his brilliant graphic arts work. His patient forbearance with our interminable email exchanges was truly breathtaking. A hearty shout-out to my husband, Mark. Thanks for your tireless love, your editing support, and for cooking dinner all those nights I couldn't tear myself away from the computer. And to Katlyn, my child, and bright North Star. Thank you for challenging me to keep asking the right questions. To my sister and brother, Kim and Brad, thanks for showing up year after year and reminding me to laugh. And finally, I am forever grateful to my mom and dad, Jean and Cliff Prodger. Both writers, I have a suspicion this book is in part their work; thanks for your kibitzing and wordsmithing from beyond the veil.

Contents

List of Diagrams

List of Exercises

Introduction

This book is written for ordinary people interested in improving their lives through spiritual awareness and the practice of simple clairvoyant exercises. I began this book in 2008 after seven years of experience working as a clairvoyant counselor in Alameda, California. Now I resume my endeavor with more than 21 years of professional clairvoyant experience and several years studying the Seth material: that lively "energy personality essence" channeled by Jane Roberts from 1963 and until her death in 1984. Those concepts learned in "psychic school" sparked my interest in the Seth material and my quest for a deeper comprehension about our multidimensional reality and the boundless capacities of the human mind.

After a few years working as an intuitive, I began to question why our Western culture is so shut-down in terms of our natural psychic functioning and the full use of our wide-ranging consciousness. Why are we disconnected from our own inner voice and deeper wellspring of spiritual insight in the first place? I will explore some cultures that not only accept, *but rely on*, spiritual insight attained through "extrasensory means." These examples provide a model and inspiration for us to reclaim our natural clairvoyant abilities, our birthright. By illuminating the differences in core beliefs and approaches, we can better understand why many of us abandoned our psychic natures in the first place. We may then circle back and bridge the psychic divide in a conscious and fully committed way.

This book is meant to inspire and assist you in reconnecting with your mystical self in a most natural and powerful way and to reclaim your psychic nature so that you may live a more integrated and fulfilling life. I have included sixteen simple exercises to help you open and strengthen communication with your inner self. This process of self-discovery will aid you in identifying limiting beliefs so you may transform them energetically. By learning how to manipulate your own energy and focus your attention clairvoyantly, you will gain a new level of spiritual perception and energetic techniques that will support your continuing growth and exploration. After playing with the concepts and exercises for a while, it will become natural to "ask yourself" the things you want to understand before you run out to consult an "expert" on *your life*. You are more than you realize, and your spiritual capacities are boundless and forever expanding. I invite you to sit down, relax, and "ask yourself" what you are curious to know. Your answers will find you.

PART ONE

Reclaiming Your Psychic Nature

Chapter 1

The Power of Play

True creativity comes from enjoying the moments, which then
fulfill themselves, and a part of the creative process is indeed
the art of relaxation, the letting go, for that triggers magical
activity...
–Seth, *Magical Approach* (Roberts 8)

I grew up in a time when kids were allowed to play freely outdoors; no helicopter parents, recreational electronics, or fear of abductions. We played in the sunshine with our friends, tearing through the neighborhood armed only with our imaginations. The standing rule was when the streetlights turned on, it was time to go inside. I was extremely fortunate to grow up in the 1960s in Southern California –Thousand Oaks to be exact. Those were the days when oak trees really did outnumber the commercial developments in the Conejo Valley. The rolling hills, dotted with prickly pear cacti and those magnificent oaks, were the perfect playground for a kid. Luckier still, our neighborhood was out in the middle of "nowhere" but still within walking distance to the television sets constructed for the TV Westerns, *Gunsmoke* and *The Rifleman*. We could play for hours, creating every sort of scenario, and never get bored. Parents were more relaxed then, happy to get their kids outside to "blow-off steam." Dad's attentive parenting style was summed up by his favorite directive as we ran out the door, "Watch out for the rattlers!" (Nobody was ever bitten.)

I remember, later in my adolescence, I spent many hours exploring the hills near our new home in Newbury Park, our second residence a few miles from Thousand Oaks. I had several favorite trees in which I climbed to perch for some afternoon daydreaming. I gave each tree a name and they were more than just perches; they were my friends. I felt awkward as a teenager, but not in the hills or with the trees. Those long walks in nature always relaxed me and provided a sense of balance and calm. Once I fell asleep in the long grass on a hill. I was awakened later by the bleating of a flock of sheep peering down at me, voicing their perplexity over this random human arranged horizontally in their grazing field.

My younger days roaming the hills of southern California laid a strong foundation for my deep appreciation of nature and my need for time outdoors to recharge my soul. It also started a life-long love affair with hiking, running, bicycling, camping (and old Westerns). I wasn't aware until more recently that these are not just random preferences. It's how I redirect my energy and get unstuck when my life becomes too pressured or out of balance. I can breathe, reground and slip back into the present moment just as naturally as a child engaged in spontaneous play. I learned this at a very early age and rely on it to this day: moving my body outside in nature works every time to redirect a negative mindset or uplift a troubled day.

Looking back, my most memorable play-time experience was when I was about seven years old. I was playing with my best friend, Kimmy, on the grounds of the church at the corner of our street. I don't remember exactly what we were playing, but I recall it had something to do with hidden treasure. Kimmy and I combed the rocky hillside below the parking lot of the church. I called out that I had found the treasure. I pointed and proclaimed, "There's a quarter under that rock!" I remember being completely exhilarated by this prospect and 100 percent certain it was true, even before I looked. Kimmy approached me and we overturned the rock only to find a bright, shining quarter beneath it! I will never forget the magical feeling that thrilled through my body. I was sure that quarter would be there and it was. We glowed at each other as though we'd discovered a pot of gold buried on the hillside by the church.

This was my first memorable psychic experience and it changed my life. As a kid, play and magic went hand-in-hand. I discovered that when I was immersed in the flow of play and I *knew something with 100% certainty*, magical experiences would unfold as a matter of course. *I often knew things even before physical evidence validated them as true.* It was as if my inner self was whispering in my ear, "There is more going on here than the grown-ups are talking about. Keep playing and expect magic."

The irony of this memory is that at the same church on the corner of our street, I attended a Bible study lesson that year. I remember the teacher instructing our small group of young kids that if you put a Bible on the ground, you will go to hell and burn forever for this "transgression." She also offered variations on this theme for us to memorize. For example, if you stack a Bible with other books and the Bible is on the bottom, you will also go to hell. There were about four or five similar rules to memorize and adhere to your entire life if you were to be saved from the terrible fate of burning in hell. As you can imagine, I was paralyzed with fear. I remember running back home to recite the rules to my mother so we could write them down before I forgot. As I approached our house, I was sure I had forgotten at least a few of them. I could hardly breathe, and my entire world contracted into a frozen state of terror. When I got home, I found my mom and blurted out as many of the rules as I could remember. She was appalled at what I had been told at Bible study and assured me that those rules were absolutely false. She reminded me that because she was "the mom" her knowledge trumped all others. Well, who could argue with that? And what a relief. I was lucky to have been raised by my mom. How differently my perspective could have been shaped had she not helped me challenge those frightening messages taught that afternoon. Needless to say, I was never sent to that children's study group ever again.

I am struck by the powerful contrast of experiences I had at that church in my seventh year. One, expansive and magical as we played in a spontaneous flow of creative activity. The other, restrictive, fearful and paralyzing—where my power and perspective dissolved in the condemning authority of a perfect stranger. These two experiences presented a potent contrast of approaches for me to consider over the years. Even now as an adult it is one of the most critical considerations I make on a daily basis: the choice to live spontaneously and in the flow of my own true self, *or* within a framework of externally imposed beliefs and conditions. In large part, that is what this book is about.

Through my four years of clairvoyant training as well as the exploration of the "subtle self" of thousands of people I have "read" since, I have caught glimpses of a new road map of human consciousness and our multi-dimensional self. One which transcends any strictly rational and materialist model of reality and instead affirms our subtle inner experience, wisdom, and energetic connection to all things.

In *The Magical Approach*, Seth says, "The old beliefs, of course, and the rational approach, are everywhere reinforced, and so it does indeed have a great weight. The magical approach has far greater weight, if you use it and allow yourselves to operate in that fashion, for it has the weight of your basic natural orientation. The rational approach is the superimposed one" (Roberts, *Magical Approach* 9-10). Please join me in this "magical" quest. Together, we will discover lost parts of ourselves and experience new vistas of consciousness and creativity.

The following grounding exercise is a wonderful practice to do outside in your yard or in nature. It is just as effective when done indoors, however, and is beneficial to do every day. Grounding helps you to feel safe and centered during your day and release unneeded energy and anxiety from your body and aura. It also helps you to balance your energy so it is optimal for your body and in resonance with the earth. Finally, the exercise will instruct you in how to draw fresh earth energy in through the secondary chakras on the bottom of your feet. This replenishes you and helps stabilize your system. I recommend you record the exercises in this book into your phone or a digital recorder. You can then play them back to use as guided meditations.

Exercise 1
Grounding Your Energy System to the Earth

*Sit in a straight back chair and allow your feet to rest flat on the ground. Take a few deep, relaxing breaths and allow yourself to settle into your body. Imagine your worries and any distractions simply floating away. Close your eyes and turn your attention inward.

*Visualize a ball of green light spinning at the base of your spine, perhaps the size of a softball. Relax and watch it spin. Set the intention that this ball will attract and absorb all of your stress and any stagnant energy held in your aura and body. Feel tight spots in your body let go and relax and send the tension down into this spinning green ball.

*After a few moments relaxing and visualizing the green ball, release it and allow it to fall down to the center of the planet. As it falls, visualize a cord of equal diameter trailing behind it, still attached to the base of your spine. *This is your grounding cord.*

*Imagine the earth accepting this ball of green light and embracing it with love. Relax and notice the difference you feel when you are grounded to the planet. Breathe deeply and enjoy the calming, stabilizing sensations of grounding your body.

*Now imagine on the arch of each foot, a small chakra opening. Allow the soft, warm energy of the earth to enter your feet chakras naturally. This is effortless. It naturally flows gently into your feet, up your legs and into your body. The neutral vibration of earth energy nourishes your body and calms your emotions.

*Finally, notice your grounding cord continue to release old energy and worries down to the center of the planet. An energy loop is created so that you are releasing old energy down your grounding cord and pulling in fresh earth energy through your feet.

*Relax for a few moments and just breathe. Enjoy the peaceful calm of earth energy and your relationship with the planet. Thank yourself and the earth for this experience.

HOT TIPS

I can't stress this enough: go out in nature and play! If you like hiking, then hike. If you like running, then run. Spending some time in the natural world is deeply restorative and will return you to yourself. The Japanese practice of *shinrin-yoku,* which means "forest bathing" or "taking in the atmosphere," emerged in the 1980s as a way to offer relief to the burn-out associated with the 1980s techboom and resulting fatigue. Forest bathing is both physiologically and psychologically beneficial as proven by research conducted in the 1990s. But we knew that all along and only need to carve out some time for this important "ecotherapy" (Fitzgerald).

> *"In every walk with nature, one receives far more than they seek."*
> *–John Muir*

Chapter 2

Reconnecting with Your Inner Self: Reawakening Clairvoyance

When we try to pick out anything by itself,
we find it hitched to everything else in the universe.
–John Muir

Like many of my friends, I headed to college when I was 18; California State University at Chico to be exact. It was a very long drive to visit home, so I eagerly awaited the holidays for a visit with my family. When the holidays finally arrived and I returned home, I took a walk back out to the hills to visit my favorite trees. Instead, I found a new housing tract development. The entire area had been regraded, paved and not a single hill, field or tree remained. I was shocked, heartbroken and enraged all at once and the memory saddens me even now. Within only a few months my natural retreat and personal sanctuary had been completely eliminated from the face of the planet. The weight of that loss moved me in a lasting and profound way. It *did* help me to choose a major, however—a decision that had eluded me since entering college: Environmental Studies. After one and a half years at CSU Chico, I transferred to the University of California Santa Cruz which offered a top-notch Environmental Studies program.

After receiving my bachelor's degree in 1983 from UCSC, I pursued the environmental field for 15 years as a program developer and grant writer for multiple natural resource conservation organizations. In my 20s, I established an employment training program in Santa Cruz County which obtained government and private grant funding for stream and fisheries restoration, watershed protection and natural resource education programs. I went on to help establish another conservation corps program in San Jose, CA and to obtain similar conservation funding for local watersheds, park land fisheries and nature education programs.

And, though I appreciate the importance of this work, one day it dawned on me that environmental degradation is, at its core, a spiritual problem. The only way people could possibly overlook the immense importance of living in balance with the planet is if they are disconnected from their own true spiritual nature and the earth. I believe this lack of awareness and concern stems from living constantly in a dissociated state, both physically and spiritually. Humans have set themselves apart from the natural world, presume a superior status, and "use nature" rather than live in balance with it, as a part of it. In fact, the very term "environmental" implies something separate and outside oneself. The result of this separatist perspective is climate change, over population, deforestation, pollution and loss of natural habitat for thousands of species threatening their extinction, to name only a few of the urgent issues. As Lynn McTaggart wrote in her book, *The Bond: How to Fix your Falling-Down World*:

> But the crises we face on many fronts are symptomatic of a deeper problem, with more potential repercussions than those of any single cataclysmic event. They are simply a measure of the vast disparity between our definition of ourselves and our truest essence. For hundreds of years we have acted against nature by ignoring our essential connectedness and defining ourselves as separate from our world. We've reached a point where we can no longer live according to this false view of who we really are (McTaggart, *The Bond* xvii).

I do believe that when we humans are living in alignment with our own true spiritual nature and are open to guidance from our soul selves, we are in touch with an innate knowingness about our rightful place on the planet. We *care* rather than behave automatically and without conscience.

With this epiphany came a change in my career path. In 1998, I began training in spiritual healing and energy work as a way of approaching these problems at their roots. I wanted to understand why and how we became disconnected from our spiritual nature and our rightful place in the web of life. How is this condition reflected in the human energy system? My mission became discovering the root causes for this condition and how it might be addressed energetically. By clearing a client's energy and assisting in releasing unconscious, false beliefs and resultant energetic congestion, a person's system resets, and they return to themselves and their truth in present time.

In 1998, I was attuned in Usui Reiki and began an intensive training program in earth energy healing techniques. I was fascinated with the human energy system and found that I had a knack for hands-on healing. After an energetic healing session, my clients would comment that they felt lighter, more balanced both physically and mentally. Well, one thing led to another, and I pursued roughly four years of intensive training and apprenticing in clairvoyance. I enrolled in Aesclepion Healing Center in January 2001, one of the Bay Area's Clairvoyant Training Programs located in Marin, California. Later, I attended Psychic Horizons in San Francisco for both clairvoyant training and one year of apprenticeship. (Please note that all the Bay Area clairvoyant training programs spun off from the original Berkeley Psychic Institute founded by the late Lewis Bostwick in 1973. He must be credited for developing the clairvoyant techniques employed by all of the schools and establishing the first West Coast clairvoyant training model.)

I knew that honing my psychic abilities would assist me in becoming a better hands-on energy healer. Tracking physical or emotional problems back to their original source brought me face-to-face with the spiritual aspect of our being—the part of ourselves which is eternal and complete, and that stores all of our experiences and lessons in this life and all the others. I found that if clients had a recurring problem or pattern in their lives, the source could be found recorded in their energetic system: the chakras and the aura. I learned to "read" the chakras and the aura clairvoyantly. I learned how the energetic system functions and how people can free themselves from stuck patterns by working on this deeper, spiritual level. Looking back on that decision, I find it funny that I thought I was simply going to learn a set of techniques for such and such a purpose and carry on with my life as usual. What really happened was that my entire worldview blew apart. I began discovering how things really work, that we are spiritual beings first and foremost, and that our consciousness creates our reality and experience. It completely changed me, my understanding of the nature of reality, and my approach in the world. I am so glad I took that step, though I would never be the same. A few years later I discovered the Seth material and began reading voraciously. Who is Seth?

SETH, ESP AND "INNER ABILITIES"

In 1963, Jane Roberts of Elmira, New York, began to communicate with "Seth" who identified himself as an "energy personality essence" no longer "focused in physical form" (Roberts, *Seth Speaks* vii). Seth shared that he had experienced multiple incarnations but was no longer engaged in the reincarnational process on earth. That he was, instead, a teacher who spoke to us from the non-physical dimensions. Jane's husband, Robert Butts, participated in these communications and took verbatim notes. Over time, these meetings evolved into trance medium channeling sessions, wherein Seth began to speak directly through Jane, delivering information regarding a myriad of fascinating topics such as the nature of reality, probable universes, reincarnation, multidimensional consciousness, health, and dreams. It's impossible to impart even the smallest bit of wisdom Seth presents through Jane Roberts, so I encourage you to read this material starting with *Seth Speaks: The Eternal Validity of the Soul.* (Please refer to Other Resources section at the end of this book.) The Seth material is a tremendous information resource and catalyst for "remembering." As Plato posited, "We do not learn; and what we call learning is only a process of recollection." When I am reading the Seth material, I have a deep sense of resonance and familiarity. You will find many Seth quotes throughout this book which help illuminate my key concepts. Please note that these quotes are all statements made by Seth, channeled through Jane Roberts from 1963 to 1984. For the sake of brevity, however, I will refer to the source as "Seth" (rather than "Seth as channeled through Jane Roberts").

Seth says,

First of all, a soul is not something that you have. It is what you are... The trouble is that you consider the soul or entity as a finished, static 'thing' that belongs to you but is not you. The soul or entity—in other words, your most intimate powerful inner identity—is and must be forever changing. It is not, therefore, something like a cherished heirloom. It is alive, responsive, curious. It forms the flesh and the world that you know, and it is in a state of becoming (Roberts, *Seth Speaks* 70-1).

He explains that we are overly identified with our ego—the level of ourselves we consider the personality—or the aspect which is engaged in the physical world. Because we are conditioned to fixate exclusively on the material world and our actions within it, we have a distorted perspective; our "soul self" is regarded as something separate, different from who we are, and removed from our immediate experience. But Seth explains, "Channels, psychological and psychic, always exist, sending communications back and forth through the various levels of the self, and the ego accepts necessary information and data from inner portions of the personality without question" (Roberts, *Seth Speaks* 71). We are simply unaware of these constant communications as they take place to inform and direct our conscious personality as we move through physical reality.

This is the first thing I learned as a clairvoyant student: that we are not just physical bodies with an associated ego/personality, but that there are multiple dimensions of the self and we are first and foremost, *spirit*, a soul self, engaged in a physical experience. Our personality is but one portion of our entire, multi-dimensional personhood. Clairvoyant training, in large part, is simply opening up to that reality and beginning to communicate with those aspects of one's inner self in a conscious, focused way. The process of learning these techniques is not mysterious or even hard to master because this communication is completely natural. We have simply stopped talking, and consciously listening, to the inner portion of our beings.

If you catch yourself perceiving information through other than your physical senses, then you must accept the fact that this is the way perception works.

What happens is that your conception of reality is so limited that you take fright whenever you perceive any experience that does not fit into your conception. Now I am not speaking merely of abilities loosely called 'extrasensory perception.' These experiences seem extraordinary to you only because you have for so long denied the existence of any perception that did not come through the physical senses (Roberts, *Seth Speaks* 78).

I love this quote. Clairvoyance, clairaudience, precognition, telepathy, telekinesis, remote viewing, psychometry, mediumship, and all other "extrasensory abilities" aren't extra at all. We have simply suppressed them to fit in with the cultural norm. Our common belief here in the Western world is that none of these abilities exist or are valid experiences. At worst you are unstable psychologically and at best you suffer from an over-active imagination. As children, our psychic experiences were often invalidated. We might have been humiliated or even punished for sharing them with others. Eventually, we learned that it's best to turn our attention away from them altogether. Instead, we focus only on the physical environment and senses—those experiences upon which we can all agree.

The first few months of clairvoyant training (CT) deal with cleaning house, so to speak. We learn how to release old programming and blocks regarding our psychic senses and reawaken our sleeping abilities. The pineal gland is the seat of psychic perception and it is located at the geographic center of the head. It is usually congested energetically and its clairvoyant function shut down. It needs to be cleared to restore its natural psychic functioning.

I remember when I began this process in 2001, I detected the faintest flickering of images in fast motion. It's hard to describe. I wasn't seeing the images visually per se, but I was sensing them and they seemed to shuffle and flicker; millions of images moving at a very high speed just above my eyes. My instructor at Aesclepion reassured me that sometimes a student can perceive these "pictures" subtly as they are leaving one's energy field. He explained that our spiritual selves store information about our experiences in the form of "energetic pictures" which are held in one's energy field (the aura, or as Seth terms it, the "tissue capsule"). Not everyone has that same flickering experience as they leave the energy field, but I remember it clearly. I was astonished at the tremendous volume of images flickering above my eyes at the center of my forehead. The exercise I learned in psychic school was instrumental in clearing blocks to my clairvoyance. We would visualize a ball of golden energy in the center of the head, and gradually expand it outward to push all conges-tion out of our pineal gland, and finally our auras. The pictures cleared were of many things—mainly energetic snapshots of my past experiences being invalidated for reporting my "extrasensory" experiences to others. Some were commonly shared "cultural pictures" condemning psychic perception as false, the product of mental illness or of evil. Well, those pictures are all gone now, but the experience lasted an entire weekend for me. By Monday morning, I experienced a new heightened awareness and sharpened senses. Colors were more brilliant and every moment was crisp and alive. It was like a veil had been lifted from me.

Diagram 1 illustrates the location of the pineal gland in the head. I encourage you to study the diagram and then try Exercise 2, "Clearing Blocks from Your Psychic Center." This practice is beneficial before any kind of meditation or intuitive work because it activates the inner senses and is very centering.

Diagram 1
Center of the Head: Psychic Headquarters

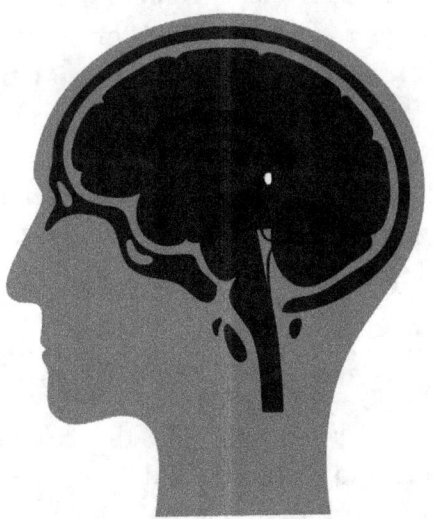

The pineal gland, shown above in white, is located
in the center of the head. It is "psychic headquarters"
and the seat of clairvoyance.

Exercise 2
Clearing Blocks from Your Psychic Center

*Sit comfortably in a straight back chair with your feet flat on the ground. Close your eyes and take a few cleansing breaths. Notice your body relaxing more and more deeply. Feel the sensation of your rear on the seat, the temperature of the air on your skin, the feeling of your hands resting lightly in your lap. Be present in the moment.

*Now, find the geographic center of your head. Imagine a line traveling from between your eyebrows straight through the back of your head. Then imagine another line starting from the top of one ear and passing through your head and out the other side, passing over the opposite ear. Where these two lines intersect is the center of your head. Find it now and rest your awareness there.

*Visualize a dot of soft golden energy at the center of your head. Visualize it growing to the size of a walnut, and then even larger... to the size of an orange. Keep watching it grow and expand, gently pushing out any old energy or "pictures" that block you from using your clairvoyance. See the golden energy lightly pulsing and growing so that it is the size of your head, continuing to gently clear your pineal gland of energetic congestion. Visualize it expanding out around your head, growing larger still.

*Give yourself the positive suggestion that all unwanted beliefs and blocking energy are clearing out of your entire aura (three to four feet beyond your body). See the golden light expand beyond your aura and release the old energy out of your space completely. Keep breathing and relaxing. Pause for a moment as the energy releases.

*Now imagine the cleansed golden light beginning to shrink back down, slowly and gently. Pulling back into your aura, back into your head, back down to the size of an orange and then a walnut. See it stabilize at about the size of a marble and glow gently at the center of your head, activating your pineal gland and opening the doors of your inner perception. You may leave the golden light glowing there even after you finish the exercise.

*When you are ready, gently bring your awareness back to the room and open your eyes. Validate yourself for clearing blocks in your psychic center and for reclaiming your clairvoyant space.

You might notice that practicing this exercise not only clears your pineal gland and sixth chakra, but it also clears your seventh chakra at the top of your head. The crown chakra is also a major spiritual center and can contain old programming and foreign energy just like the sixth chakra. I recommend doing the grounding exercise in Chapter One and this "Clearing Blocks from your Psychic Center" exercise every day. This practice will help activate your natural clairvoyance and also your crown chakra—the portal to your soul, your truth, and the non-physical dimensions.

Learning to travel to the center of your head at will is very helpful when you're experiencing a stressful event or need a higher perspective on matters. It is a neutral sanctuary available to you anytime and anywhere. Grounding to the planet and clearing your energy will help you refresh and rebalance your body and energy system. Use these exercises daily and notice how they change your life.

Now that you have begun clearing blocks to your spiritual centers—the sixth and seventh chakras at your forehead and crown respectively—you will begin to wake up your natural psychic sensing. It's helpful to learn the definitions of the various kinds of psychic abilities as there are many.

This book focuses on clairvoyance (and more specifically, reading the aura for the purpose of healing), but there are even multiple types of clairvoyance. The following glossary of terms will help you distinguish one form of psychic functioning from the other and understand the terminology more clearly. While this is not an exhaustive list and there are some differences in opinion about how they should be defined, it provides a good start to understanding the fascinating world of psychic phenomena.

Astral Travel

Also known as Out of Body Experience (OBE). The Projection of the energetic counterpart of one's self–the astral body–out of the physical body for explorations via one's mobile consciousness.

Automatic Writing

Writing while in a dissociated state, often considered communications from the writer's inner self/soul or channeled from spirit guides.

Bilocation

The presence of a person simultaneously in two different locations via paranormal means; often thought to involve an astral double.

Clairalience

The extrasensory ability to smell scents not actually present physically. We commonly hear reports of a person "smelling cigar smoke" or "perfume" while experiencing a "haunted" location.

Clairaudience

Extrasensory perception of sound; the ability to hear beyond the reach of ordinary experience or auditory capacity. Clairaudience is the French word for "clear hearing" and often involves perceiving voices and sounds from the spirit realm.

Clairsentience

Also known as the "empathic" ability, this extrasensory perception involves feeling the emotions of others. The term was also traditionally used to cover general extrasensory perceptions besides clairvoyance and clairaudience.

Clairvoyance

This French term means "clear seeing" and includes the ability to perceive subtle images, energies, locations and events out of the range of ordinary physical sight, including locations and timeframes. Examples include the ability to shift to one's "inner awareness and vision" to see auras and energy, remote locations (as in remote viewing), and to "see" future events (as in precognition). Also, dowsing may be considered a form of clairvoyant sensing, but uses divining rods, pendulums or other instruments to help locate water, minerals or other objects hidden from ordinary physical sight. A more dated term for clairvoyance is "second sight" and references are often made to the "third eye" identifying this chakra at the forehead as the seat of clairvoyance.

Field Consciousness

This is an altered state of consciousness wherein a person experiences an enlargement of the ordinary boundaries of the self, merging with their environment and identifying with a more expansive sense of self and unity with "the whole."

Intuition

Also termed claircognizance, intuition is the ability to know or obtain knowledge through immediate insights rather than through reasoning or ordinary rational processes.

Levitation

To raise one's body or other objects into the air via non-physical means.

Mediumship

To perceive and communicate with the deceased. Mental mediums receive messages from people who have passed on and transmit them to the living. Trance mediumship is the ability to dissociate from one's body and allow a discarnate or spirit teacher to enter their body and speak through them directly. James Van Praagh is a medium. Edgar Cayce and Jane Roberts were trance mediums. The term "physical medium" refers to a person who, either in or out of trance, calls on spirits who can physically affect objects in the immediate location. Physical mediumship was very popular in the 19th and 20th centuries during the spiritualist movement.

Precognition

The ability to "see" the future beforehand; to foretell events prior to their occurrence. This is often thought to be another form of clairvoyance wherein the sensitive is able to shift out of linear time and clairvoyantly "see" a future event. Similarly, retrocognition is the ability to clairvoyantly "see" an historical event which occurred in the past.

Psychokinesis

Also known as telekinesis, this is the ability to affect physical matter using one's mental focus and intention. Also popularly termed mind-over-matter.

Psychometry

Also known as object reading. The sensitive holds an object and can perceive information related to the object's history through extrasensory means; often sensing details about the people and events associated with the object.

Remote Viewing

Also known as "traveling clairvoyance." This is the extrasensory ability to perceive and describe a remote or hidden target without the support of the ordinary physical senses. Remote viewing is considered one of the many forms of clairvoyance.

Telepathy

Also known as "thought transference." This is the ability to transmit thoughts and images from one person to another without using any known human sensory channels or direct physical communication. The siddhis of India categorize telepathy as another form of clairvoyance.

There is a wealth of information available on each of these psychic forms of perception. I've listed some of my favorite books in the Other Resources section at the back of this book. You may find you have a particular knack for one or more of these psychic abilities. I encourage you to explore your abilities with an expectation of mastery and success. These are innate functions and with enough time and practice, you can develop them to the extent you desire. This book will help you reawaken your clairvoyance and intuition and provides many of the same tools and exercises I used in my own training and clairvoyant development. I welcome you to your clairvoyant journey. I am excited to share some tried and true techniques I learned while traveling my own psychic path.

HOT TIPS

I have found it very helpful to have a psychic journal where I record all of my psychic experiences and exercises. I urge you to find a nice journal or notebook and begin your own. For each of the exercises in this book, you can record your experience and jot down notes about how things are going. You can also record your dreams in this journal and watch for messages from this aspect of your psyche. Periodically, I love to review my journal to see how my own unique psychic journey is unfolding in my life. I think you will be glad to have your own psychic development records too, so I encourage you to begin your journal today.

Chapter 3

The Captivity of Attention

"Ask yourself."
—Lewis Bostwick, (1918-1995)
Founder of the Berkeley Psychic Institute

After clutter-clearing the pineal gland and sixth chakra, the next task as a clairvoyant student was to become aware of the focus of our attention. From a very young age, we are trained to place our attention outside of ourselves and fix it on a parent, teacher or any grown-up requiring it. Obviously, accepting guidance from our elders is important as we "learn the ropes" of living. But our attention may become so conditioned to look outside of ourselves for guidance that we begin to lose touch with our own inner voice—the wellspring of innate wisdom coming from within. We may be humiliated in school when our attention wanders and we are reprimanded by the teacher. After years of responding to the familiar command: "give me your attention!" barked by teachers, coaches, parents and any other authority, we are conditioned to focus outwardly for direction and information. After hours upon years of fatiguing focus on the "expert," we form a habitual pattern of looking outward to others for the answers. It does not even occur to us to ask ourselves.

Obviously, in order to learn new skills and practical information it makes perfect sense to pay attention to the information imparted by others with more experience and knowledge in the areas we must learn. We are social creatures and it is in our nature to share and support one another and offer our unique knowledge and gifts to others. The problem begins when we aren't also encouraged and validated for tuning into our own intuitive information that flows continually from our inner selves. Instead, we have learned to censor and disregard it. External information overrides our inner voice and the constant urgings and intuitions sent to us from within.

My clairvoyant instructor asked us to practice focusing our awareness outwardly on him and then withdraw it back into the center of our head, back into our clairvoyant space. We were asked to notice the difference of energy, awareness and information that registers there, often in the form of images. By doing this several times we were able to increase the mobility of our attention and break the trance of our conditioned outward focus.

A core concept developed through this system of clairvoyant instruction is Lewis Bostwick's old adage, "Ask yourself." Bostwick founded the Berkeley Psychic Institute in 1973 and developed an entire system for honing one's innate clairvoyant skills and energy awareness. Bostwick posited that all information can be accessed directly through one's own spiritual channels—the sixth and seventh chakras at the forehead and crown of the head, respectively. These centers are built into our energy systems for the purpose of seeing clearly ("clairvoyance," in French) and knowing truth, the function of the crown (seventh) chakra. This concept is both simple and revolutionary. To use these "extrasensory" abilities isn't to be gifted. It is the natural functioning of the inner self, an intrinsic part of our energetic anatomy, and therefore completely available to everyone. The crown chakra is the seat of "knowingness." It is where we know what is true. When you "ask yourself" for guidance about a dilemma or for creative inspiration and direction, the crown chakra is the gateway through which the information is delivered to the conscious mind. Our inner self speaks to us, providing the information we need to resolve problems or spark creative activity. But we have become so conditioned to believe the answers are outside of ourselves, or that someone else knows better than we do, that we habitually seek answers and guidance from outside "experts" and not from our own soul.

My instructor at Aesclepion often reminded me to "ask myself" when I came to him with questions after class (annoying and empowering at the same time). The CT program introduced students to the concept of "spiritual certainty" meaning to embrace your own spiritual information and trust it. We were constantly reminded not to "give our crowns away" meaning not to subjugate our own truth to another person's information. Ask yourself, and then listen!

The following exercise will help you to call back your attention and seat it in the center of your head. The more you practice this, the better you will become at centering yourself and connecting with your own intuitive information. I urge you to do this every day for a few weeks. Then you will familiarize yourself with the subtle shift in your awareness when your attention is focused inwardly, versus externally.

Exercise 3
Calling Back Your Attention

*Sit in a straight back chair with your feet resting flat on the ground. Close your eyes and take a few deep, relaxing breaths. Tune in to the present moment.

*Bring your attention to the center of your head and clear this clairvoyant space with the gold dot of energy described in Exercise 2. Notice the neutral, calming effect of the gold vibration and its elevating effect on your awareness.

*Now gently open your eyes and fix your gaze on something interesting to you within your field of vision. Study it and acknowledge its features, color and shape. Acknowledge as many details about this object as you can within a minute or so. Imagine your attention like a ray of light emanating from your eyes and projecting outward, scanning the object of your attention.

*Now close your eyes again. Imagine that ray of light withdrawing back into your eyes. Take a few deep, restful breaths. Pull your awareness back a few more inches and seat it in the center of your head. Feel the warm glow of golden light. Experience the shift of feelings, thoughts and impressions you experience here. Let them float through your awareness and continue to breathe and simply observe them. Give yourself a minute or two to enjoy the neutral quality of your psychic center.

*Next open your eyes and fix your gaze on a different object. Repeat the exercise.

*Acknowledge the subtle inner awareness of your "clairvoyant space." Thank yourself for this experience and reground your body to the center of the planet.

With practice, you will notice the difference in vibration and quality of your awareness. It is from this place, your inward focus, you can more easily ask yourself questions and receive answers in the form of images, flashes of insight, or a knowingness that pervades your awareness. Connecting with your inner self re-establishes conscious communication with your soul, providing a channel for your soul's answers to merge with your ordinary awareness. Try this every day for a few weeks, and your inner focus will become sharp and clear.

HOT TIPS

Once you have mastered seating your attention in the center of your head, you can experiment with your eyes open. A beneficial practice is to call your attention inward to the center of your head before and during a social engagement. Many of us are empaths and are aware that we absorb other people's energy and emotions into our own energetic space. We typically think of this as another person's energy moving from their aura into our own; that we are a passive receptacle. But sometimes the opposite is true. Because energy follows attention, we often unconsciously project our energy into other people's auras during our interactions with them. Then when we leave the conversation, we unconsciously draw the merged energy back into our own aura, consequently absorbing part of their energy in the process. By staying seated in the center of your head, you can interact with people just as effectively but still maintain better personal boundaries and healthier energetic hygiene.

Chapter 4

Cultural Comparisons: Ideas Versus Visions

*An old chief of the Crow tribe from Montana was once asked
to describe the difference between his tribe and the whites who
lived nearby. Pausing slightly and drawing his conclusions, he
remarked that the white man has ideas, the Indian has visions.*
—Vine Deloria, Jr. Spirit and Reason

In this chapter, I will explore prevalent cultural barriers in the West that discourage us from acknowledging our natural psychic faculties and fully integrating extrasensory experiences into our lives. Around the globe and throughout history, there have been millions of people demonstrating legitimate psychic abilities that are valued by their communities and acknowledged openly in their cultures. We will consider some of these examples drawing from the work of Dean Radin, Ph.D (Chief Scientist for the Institute of Noetic Sciences), as well as the essays of late Native American scholar, Vine Deloria, Jr. It's hard to deny the truth about psychic phenomena when we see these authors' impressive line-up of examples from around the world. Finally, we will examine entrenched institutional resistance found here in the West—scientific, academic and religious—to help us understand why we Westerners don't readily claim and use our natural psychic abilities. When consciously acknowledging what some institutions have conditioned us to believe (and disbelieve), it frees us to make our own choices about our beliefs. Then we may reclaim our natural psychic heritage with purpose and intention.

Dean Radin, PhD, in his book *Supernormal: Science, Yoga, and the evidence for Extraordinary Psychic Abilities*, explores various psychic phenomena as demonstrated through the siddhis—the disciplined meditation practices of advanced yoga in India.

Classic yoga texts, such as Patanjali's Yoga Sutras, written about two thousand years ago, tell us in matter of fact terms that if you sit quietly, pay close attention to your mind, and practice this diligently, then you will gain supernormal powers. These advanced capacities are not regarded as magical; they're ordinary capacities that everyone possesses. We're just too distracted most of the time to be able to access them reliably (Radin 8).

This is my experience too. I participated in about four years of meditation and intensive clairvoyant training classes and found myself learning to connect with a whole new level of information, subtle energy and intuitions that were helpful for myself and others. By clearing my mind and energy field of distractions, adjusting my energy centers, and stabilizing my focus inwardly, a new world opened up to me. Clairvoyance is considered one of the more basic or garden variety psychic skills or "siddhis;" I can't levitate or become invisible (yet). These abilities are considered among the more advanced siddhis and I'm sure it takes many years of meditation and diligent training to master these forms of "supernormal powers." And to be sure, the yogis pursuing the siddhis in India adopted many lifestyle changes and advanced meditation techniques quite different than the style I learned in only four years in California. All of the students of the San Francisco Bay Area clairvoyant schools have learned at least the basic fundamentals needed to begin developing their natural clairvoyant abilities through this modern Western training model; and many in as much as only one year of meditation and training. This is a very positive proposition for Westerners who can't practically drop their lives, move to an ashram in India and adopt a completely different lifestyle. Our modern lives here in the West can still accommodate the learning and mastery of at least this particular form of clairvoyance in a relatively short period of time. The core of the clairvoyant training and mastery involves a consistent meditation practice.

I often wonder how different it would be to grow up in a culture that accepts all psychic functions as normal and a part of our natural range of perceptual abilities, albeit non-physical sensory perceptions. If we were to practice meditation and remain disciplined in our pursuit of "extrasensory abilities," then clairvoyance, telepathy, precognition, and psychokinesis—in fact any psi ability—could manifest as a matter of course. If we were as a society encouraged to focus attention on the development of these natural human abilities, they might even become commonplace.

> Psychic effects are considered ho-hum supernormal abilities that some yogis and sadhus (holy men) possess. They are understood as refined aspects of mind and consciousness that have been discussed in great depth by scholars and practitioners for millennia. Why bother studying something with the newfangled tools of science when it is already accepted as commonplace? (Radin xxi)

What exactly are the Yoga Sutras and the Siddhis in India where supernormal abilities are "ho-hum?" The Yoga Sutras were written by Patanjali of India about two thousand years ago for the purpose of synthesizing and recording the generations of oral tradition which instructed students on the principles and knowledge of Classical Yoga (Radin 96). Prior to the Yoga Sutras, knowledge was passed along through oral tradition and presentations. Now the knowledge has been organized and recorded in a document still studied today. The Yoga Sutras are made up of four books called "padas." They are: (1) *Samadhi Pada* which focuses on meditative absorption; (2) *Sadhana Pada* covers the practice of yoga; (3) *Vibhuti Pada* focuses on extraordinary abilities, known as the siddhis, that unfold when traveling the yogic path; and (4) *Kaivalya Pada*, the final book, is about yoga's ultimate goal—spiritual liberation (Radin 97). In the third book, the *Vibhuti Pada*, 25 siddhis are identified falling within the three categories of: "(1) Exceptional mind-body control; 2) Clairvoyance, the ability to gain knowledge unbound by the ordinary constraints of space or time and without the use of the ordinary senses; includes precognition and telepathy; 3) Psychokinesis—the ability of the mind to directly influence physical matter" (Radin 109). The classic siddhis are gained through disciplined and dedicated meditative practice and are proven highly reliable. Radin interprets them as extremely refined forms of psychic phenomena which are also acknowledged in other spiritual belief systems such as shamanism and the mystical branches of many religions. Though Western science and academia in large part deny these abilities are real, according to surveys, most of the world's population believe in one or more of these "superhuman abilities" (Radin 9).

Shamanism is an excellent example of accepted mystical practices central to many indigenous cultures throughout the world. Shamans have always been the keepers of wisdom, healing, and oracular information. Their tribes have relied on them to enter visionary states skillfully and on demand. Psychedelic drugs such as the Amanita muscaria mushroom have been used by shamans to induce trance states and access information not readily available via normal consciousness. Other methods used to reach these altered states of consciousness include, "music, dancing, controlled breathing, drumming, fasting, breathing intoxicating vapors, and meditation" (Radin 40). Over centuries of trial and error, methods used by shamans to enter trance states have been perfected and passed down through the ages, and from generation to generation. In this context, mystical experience is not only accepted culturally, but in a practical sense, indispensable to tribes, enabling them to survive harsh environments and circumstances.

Late Native American scholar, Vine Deloria, Jr.'s book, *Spirit and Reason,* is a brilliant collection of essays examining traditional Native American peoples' perspectives and practices ranging from education, social science, politics, philosophy and religion. Deloria, Jr. compares Western European perspectives with those of native peoples contrasting the stark differences in world view and approaches to life. It is worthwhile considering some of these differences more closely because the Native American approach demonstrates both accepted mystical experience and an implicit sense of connection and respect among people, the earth and all creatures. Native peoples' seamless integration of mystical/psychic experience demonstrate how practically useful these capacities are to the group. Furthermore, their world view and approach are based on respect for all life, supporting balance and responsible practices in the greater "living universe."

Deloria, Jr. explains that to native people everything is connected, respected, and alive. The antithesis of reductionist thinking, the native people not only feel a kinship with the natural world, but the value of this connection is recognized through all relationships and experiences. He states,

For the most part Indians do not 'deal with' or 'love' nature. In the Western European context human experience is separated from the environment. When Indians are told that they "love nature," they cannot deal with this because nature is not an abstraction to them. Indians do not talk about nature as some kind of concept or something 'out there.' They talk about the immediate environment in which they live. They do not embrace all trees or love all rivers and mountains. What is important is the relationship you have with a particular tree or a particular mountain (Deloria Jr. 223).

I am struck by another key difference in perspective. That all experience has value and is an education about some part of life. You can't "mis-experience." *You can only come away with a misinterpretation of that experience* (Deloria Jr. 46). To be open and alert as you move through life means you shouldn't "jump to conclusions" or you will miss emerging and new circumstances and fail to register important changes. Observation through experience is how knowledge is acquired, built upon and refined through time, and acted upon in practical ways. Theoretical, stand-alone information is not valued. It must be useful. Integration into daily life and decision making is the purpose of knowledge. If this isn't possible, the information is of no relevance.

In addition, "The world is constantly creating itself because everything is alive and making choices that determine the future" (Deloria Jr. 46). Because everything is related and alive, finding one's place and proper action in any circumstance is important and is indeed that person's responsibility to the whole. In this moral universe, "all activities, events, and entities are related, and consequently it does not matter what kind of existence an entity enjoys, for the responsibility is always there for it to participate in the continuing creation of reality" (Deloria Jr. 47). "We are all relatives" is a central tenet underpinning a world view that each part of the whole is important, to be respected, learned from, and cooperated with. It is a phrase heard in ceremonies and is a blessing that encompasses all life, including the plant and animal world. All experience within this alive and connected universe is instructive and builds a base of knowledge helping the tribe to live not only more comfortably in the world, but also with profound meaning in the "now" and the emerging future. "Knowledge was derived from individual and communal experiences in daily life, in keen observation of the environment, and in the interpretive messages that they received from spirits in ceremonies, visions and dreams" (Deloria Jr. 44). The method of obtaining knowledge is through direct and immediate experience, both individually and collectively, unlike Western knowledge which is largely based on abstractions and theoreticals. "An old chief of the Crow tribe from Montana was once asked to describe the difference between his tribe and the whites who lived nearby. Pausing slightly and drawing his conclusions, he remarked that the white man has ideas, the Indian has visions" (Deloria Jr. 15). This is a wonderful quote and so revealing of the profound differences in the ways we think and operate. Indigenous peoples are immersed in direct experience with the perspective that divine energy moves through all things and "reveals itself in particular objects and places." Deloria says that to deny this would be to deny an ultimate sense of reality itself. The use of recognitions, not abstract beliefs, are relied upon so that each perception engages the totality of personality.

> A truly wise and gifted individual can appear to 'cause' things to happen because that person can participate in the emerging event in a way that rarely occurs in Western science. Thus it is that people are said to have 'powers,' which is another way of saying that their understanding of natural process and their ability to enter into events are highly developed and sophisticated (Deloria Jr. 50).

A savior figure is not needed to control reality or change a circumstance. In their view, direct and immediate participation of each aspect of the universe, human and otherwise, contribute to the weaving together of reality. Deloria comments that the old Indians didn't need a "specific higher personality" who demanded worship but instead experienced "personality in every aspect of the universe and called it 'Woniya' (Spirit), looking to it for guidance" (Deloria Jr. 48).

Sometimes, specific and immediate information would be needed.

The knowledge base might need refining or very specific solutions to a new situation or problem would demand immediate illumination. Maybe this would include new illnesses or crises not addressed by the current body of knowledge possessed by tribal members.

> At certain times some men and women would receive, either in dreams or in visions, very precise knowledge on other ways in which the plant could be used by humans—information that could not have been obtained through experiment or trial and error use. Some knowledge was so precise that it might only be needed once in a lifetime. And of course tribes often shared their knowledge of plants or even traded medicinal plants back and forth across large distances so that the knowledge of plants took on an encyclopedic aspect (Deloria Jr. 53).

Beyond mystical revelations and dreams, one's relationship with immediate environment and "sacred places" are the foundation for observations and the building of knowledge. But the forced dislocation of Native American communities has caused a loss of data; natives are prevented from roaming freely over their homelands to gather plants and animals for their daily needs as well as ceremonies held at their traditional sacred sites. Therefore, building knowledge in the traditional ways—through relationship and observation on their homelands—is severely compromised (Deloria Jr. 34). The loss of Native American homelands, including sacred lands and ceremonial sites, has caused extreme dislocation in all aspects of native life. They see their ceremonies as a central responsibility—their traditional duty to the earth and "all persons" (which also includes the plant and animal kingdom)—to ensure the earth is abundant and all life can thrive. This practice has grown increasingly problematic:

> One of the primary aspects of traditional tribal religions has been the secret ceremonies, particularly vision quests, the fasting in the wilderness, and the isolation of the individual for religious purposes. This type of religious practice is nearly impossible today. The places currently available to people for vision quests are

hardly isolated. Jet planes pass overhead. Some traditional holy places are the scene of strip-mining, others are adjacent to super-highways, others are parts of ranches, farms, shopping centers and natural parks and forests (Deloria Jr. 315).

The fracturing of traditional native life through the piece-by-piece dissolution of their living universe imperils the very fabric of their world and brilliant ways of moving through it. To me, it also represents a tragic lost opportunity for non-indigenous peoples to learn more respectful and responsible ways to live in balance on the planet. Our disconnection from the natural world gives rise to a separatist perspective which fails to value our connection and responsibility within the whole of life. Deloria, Jr. states, "The living universe requires mutual respect among its members...The willingness of entities to allow others to fulfill themselves, and the refusal of any entity to intrude thoughtlessly on another, must be the operative principle of this universe" (Deloria Jr. 50-51). A central attitude is that if we want to obtain benefits from the earth and her creatures, it cannot be obtained at the expense of other creatures or the earth itself. This is "shortsighted and disrupts the balance that the whole fabric of life requires" (Deloria Jr. 51).

Learning some of these native principles and living with an attitude of respect on the earth would help us to embody our true essence and find our rightful place within the web of life. Maybe then we would adopt more sustainable ecological practices with greater discipline and commitment. We have also seen how shamanic and Native American spiritual traditions provide an extremely potent example of mystical practices that support communities of people both practically and spiritually.

In addition to the siddhis of India, all shamanistic and Native American traditions, Radin also cites examples of supernormal powers found throughout the mystical branches of many religions. The Catholic charisms of the West lists multiple saints who have performed extraordinary psychic feats. Clairvoyance, precognitive abilities, and "miraculous" healings and cures have been performed by a number of saints including Saint Gertrude, Saint Hildegard, Saint Birgitta of Sweden, Saint Catherine of Siena, and Saint Teresa (Radin 62). But the extraordinary psychic demonstrations don't end there. Between 200 and 300 historical cases of levitation have been reported, including those of Saint Joseph of Cupertino (1603–1663). St. Joseph was frequently witnessed levitating and many of these cases were officially recorded in depositions provided under oath by more than 150 eyewitnesses including popes, kings and princesses (Radin 62).

Some other religions mentioned are the *Karāmāts* (supernatural wonders performed by Muslim saints) of the Islamic religion; the divination practices of *zaddiks* in Judaism; and the *ngön she* (heightened awareness) in Tibetan Buddhism (Radin 61). Together, all of these examples provide compelling evidence of what the West has persistently and vehemently denied: that multiple forms of psychic phenomena are, beyond doubt, real. So, why are we in the West so resistant to this fact?

Let's consider some of the institutional barriers that interfere with the acceptance of psychic phenomena in the Western world. Much of Radin's book focuses on scientific experiments and their findings regarding a range of psychic phenomena: precognition, telepathy, psychokinesis in both living and inanimate systems, clairvoyance, and meditation. The institutions of science and academia in the West have traditionally denied the legitimacy of extrasensory abilities and psychic phenomena. Taking any of these abilities seriously and spending the time and funds to research them is rare and even taboo. It is true that throughout time there have been many psychic fakes employing deceptive techniques. If you are skeptical to begin with, those displays are enough to convince you that the entire range of psychic phenomena is false. Additional unbiased laboratory testing of psychic phenomena using reliable methodology is needed to dispel false information and shine a true light on what is really happening. However, scientific and academic circles resist undertaking these experiments and exploring psychic phenomena with an open mind. In Radin's words:

> If my belief based on evidence is true, even to the slightest degree, then the skeptical house of cards falls apart. The skeptics position, after all, is that absolutely nothing interesting is going on, despite admissions...that the cumulative evidence actually is persuasive. Given this asymmetry, the professional skeptic must continue to deny or ignore all positive evidence because

otherwise the 'sunk cost' of an entire career is at stake. That's a heavy burden to bear when the evidence just keeps on getting stronger (Radin 88).

Science and academia have a lot invested—indeed the entire structure of accepted scientific beliefs regarding the nature of reality and human potential is at stake here.

Besides institutional resistance, there are other hurdles to navigate when undertaking research in psi phenomena. Radin explains that trying to prove some of these paranormal abilities in tightly controlled experimental settings can be tricky.

If we are interested in phenomena where we want high confidence that what we're studying is real, rather than a mistake, a coincidence, or one or more perceptual biases, then we must turn to controlled laboratory experiments. Lab studies don't explore the raw, messy, everyday world at large. They investigate, usually with tight controls, artificially constrained versions of the real world.

The price for gaining high confidence in these observations is that we have to narrow our focus and define the boundaries of what we're examining. In so doing, the effects that we end up seeing in the lab tend to be tiny as compared to what happens outside the lab. This is especially true when we're studying spontaneous human behavior (Radin 120-21).

Yet he points out that some of the siddhis *are* suited for laboratory study because they *can* be scientifically assessed. Clairvoyance, precognition and extraordinary mind-body effects can deliver more verifiable results. Still, the most advanced Buddha-level masters of the siddhis usually aren't willing to go to a laboratory for examination. In the esoteric practices of India, this is strongly discouraged because such public displays are considered "showing off" and therefore discouraged (Radin 121). He reports that those studied are usually people who have some ability and have been studied in the lab before; those who have some meditation and yoga experience; but mostly volunteers who may or may not be skilled and experienced in any of the above. Unfortunately, this means that the results of many of these tests can be extremely watered down. Scientific and academic circles may interpret these weak lab findings as validation that these abilities don't really exist, thereby contributing to their persistent skepticism. Still Radin tracks numerous laboratory experiments in psi phenomena—and also presents some of his own experiments—finding both produce compelling evidence that precognition, telepathy, psychokinesis and clairvoyance *are real*. He walks us through many of these experiments and explains the protocols and findings in ways that reveal what many scientists have long resisted acknowledging: *something very interesting is indeed going on here.* "*So far, we've learned that there are rational, evidence-based reasons to accept that some of the siddhis— the ones that have been repeatedly tested under controlled conditions—are real*" (Radin 283). Though found to be rare and inconsistent in the general population—perhaps because of the inherent limitations in laboratory testing previously discussed—the findings *do validate* that these "supernormal" abilities are legitimate as proven through the scientific findings of multiple psi experiments.

Historically, the prevailing attitude has been condemning and arrogant. I'm guessing it will take time for the scientific community to accept this fact and openly acknowledge this astounding paradigm shift. Some exceptional scientists have openly acknowledged this all along. Albert Einstein always maintained that "mystical realizations" are an essential way we can grasp information not accessible through ordinary, rational means. Intuitive insights are a legitimate way the human mind can rise above ordinary thought and spark new breakthroughs in understanding (Radin 50). I hope that with time Einstein's perspective becomes the norm and that "mystical realizations" become recognized as a valid way of attaining breakthroughs in science and all other areas of discovery.

Denying the reality of psychic phenomena is persistent in Western scientific and academic communities, as we just reviewed. But what of Western religion? Are psychic experiences accepted as authentic and regarded as beneficial? Examples of supernormal powers can be found throughout many religions, including the Catholic charisms. But the Catholic religion emphasizes these are the extraordinary abilities of the saints, and saints alone. That the "gifts" are divinely bestowed by God to the few, not abilities that the ordinary person could develop through meditation and yoga. The demonstration of super-human abilities could just as well be inspired by evil forces seeking to lead the righteous astray.

> Indeed, those who display the siddhis within religious contexts are considered blessed with the divine or cursed by the demonic. This ambivalence presents a problem for how religious author-ities respond to reports of supernormal events, because the interpretation becomes as much of a political act as one of moral discernment. Witnessing a supernormal event can be powerfully seductive, and that presents a threat to traditional authority... By contrast, yoga takes a more pragmatic approach to displays of the siddhis because they are not considered divine, nor are they as tightly wound into the power struggles that seem to be endemic in all human affairs, including organized religions (Radin 61-2).

Several years ago, I took a parapsychology class from Loyd Auer-bach at JFK University in Orinda, CA. We studied research findings in parapsychology (especially regarding psychokinesis), conducted various psychic experiments in class, and read his book *Mind Over Matter: A Com-prehensive Guide to Discovering your Psychic Powers*. Auerbach speaks to the difficult topic of attributing the cause or "origin" of psychic powers by those demonstrating paranormal abilities throughout history. Because the religious perspective is that these powers are either divinely bestowed by God as in the case of the saints, or the devil's interference for the purpose of leading the righteous astray, it is a tricky subject for those psychics who display their powers publicly. I quote Auerbach:

> ...As time marched on, a person manifesting such abilities as healing or moving objects or levitation has typically stayed with the divine, believing and stating God's will is behind the phe-nomena (a safe position to declare) or that spirits of other sorts

(usually the recently departed) are helping the individual along, as with the case of mediums in the spiritualist era.

Strangely enough, those throughout history who have taken responsibility for their own extraordinary feats have been most chastised or ostracized (or, in Western history, killed as witches and sorcerers). For if the outside, socially accepted power of God (or spirits in the case of spiritualism) is not responsible, the power must come from some evil source, such as demons or Satan himself.

Anything to avoid acceptance that people, themselves, are capable of extraordinary things (Auerbach 60).

Auerbach also discussed psychological factors that have been found to help or hinder spontaneous displays of psychokinesis (PK). Kenneth Batcheldor, the late British researcher, posited that we all have "ownership resistance" of PK because it is out of the range of what is considered "normal," and people generally don't like being categorized as odd. They will exhibit resistance to owning their own abilities and demonstrating them. I wonder if subconscious religious fears also play a part in ownership resistance. If a person doesn't own and use their ability publicly, there can be no risk of condemnation from religious authorities who might claim their psychic powers are the work of evil forces. Batcheldor also found that in settings such as seances where the participants are all expecting a paranormal event and those events could be attributed to some external force besides themselves, the probability of PK events increased. Ownership resistance would be low because something or someone else was responsible for the psychic occurrence. "Witness inhibition is not a problem because the setting is one in which one expects odd things to happen (like people expecting to see a miracle from a saint whose reputation states 'miracles happen when s/he is around')" (Auerbach 66). His main point is about responsibility. "If all such reported events and abilities were considered normal, as the exceptional ability of a great athlete, we would see both more incidences of such abilities showing publicly in people, as well as a lesser need to revere—or fear—that miraculous person" (Auerbach 66).

In March 2017, I received a letter from someone signing as "Veritus," addressed to my private practice in Alameda, CA. I would have loved to respond and chat with this person, but they left no real name or contact information to make a balanced discourse possible. The gross misunderstanding about my intuitive practice was apparent throughout the four-page letter. I was struck by the misinformation "Veritus" had about modern clairvoyant counseling and what exactly transpires during a session. "Veritus" warned me that my work is an abomination and that the Bible says I should "be stoned to death for communing with evil spirits." Here are a few excerpts from the letter:

> The name of your business is "Intuitive Counseling & Healings," but where does your intuition come from? Is your mind different from the rest of ours, or do you know someone on the other side of the veil? If the ladder [sic] is true, what is the price for the information you're getting? Is it friendship or something else much more sinister? Who is your spiritual guide? Is he/she serving your Creator?
>
> Please keep in mind a few things. The devil is the father of lies. He can masquerade as an angel of light or a deceased human being. He and his legions have walked this earth since the dawn of time. That means they know things no human can know. They're keenly aware of the likes and dislikes of the departed. They know their secrets and will share them for a price—a human soul.
>
> As you have read, God considers the work that you do to be an abomination, because you are in communion with evil spirits and you are not seeking God.

I include this excerpt because it provides a keen example of the misinformation disseminated by the branches of some religions about clairvoyance and intuitive work. There seems to be a general lack of understanding regarding the many forms of mystical practice and a failure to differentiate between them. Today, the term "psychics" has been adopted popularly and lumps together all mystical practitioners. Together we are all condemned without a closer examination of our specific practices and exactly what we do. These misinformed, fear-based attitudes generate confusion and mistrust in people, discouraging them from a deeper exploration of their own innate psychic abilities.

The Bible does contain multiple warnings against the righteous being led astray by wizards, necromancers, enchanters, Chaldeans, soothsayers and witches. While being a bit murky regarding what precisely those terms meant back in ancient biblical times, I think it's safe to say they were considered nefarious and some even akin to black magic. However, clairvoyance has nothing to do with black magic, casting spells and enchantments, or colluding with demons. It is about standing in the higher (causal) dimension of one's personhood to grasp a greater comprehension of *self* and *what is*. To develop one's full range of consciousness, including clairvoyance, is simply to embody and use all of one's natural spiritual attributes. It is the human design. *Our systems have built-in subtle perceptual faculties so we may "see clearly" and discern, for ourselves, what is true.* To use one's psychic abilities is not to practice any kind of magic; it is natural, practically useful, and our birthright.

Meditation, contemplation, and the exploration of mystical experience can generate fear in our Western churches because it is different in approach than traditional Christian prayer and invites spontaneous spiritual experience. It may feel suspect because it is not instructed by doctrine or guided by church clergy. Feeling a sense of uneasiness or apprehension toward a new practice coming from a foreign land is understandable and even human. When meditation arrived on the scene in the West with Transcendental Meditation (TM) brought here by Maharishi Mahesh Yogi, I remember it caused quite a stir. Some church leaders forbade their members from participating, believing Eastern meditation is unChristian and even spiritually dangerous. I remember some even called TM satanic and Maharishi Mahesh Yogi a satanic cult leader. Through the years, traditional Western religions have resisted incorporating some of the more Eastern-inspired meditation practices, even prohibiting members from yoga or what was at the time, new practices coming from other (non-Christian) parts of the world.

But as spiritual seekers in the West have steadily integrated these practices, they have become more accepted and commonplace. Popular opinion has moved beyond rigid thinking and pushed back on dogmatic religious restrictions. I see this as an evolution of awareness and accep-tance regarding mystical experience. People have gained more facility in meditation and reaped the benefits of their own personal transcendent experiences. With this new confidence, many are more willing to chal-lenge reactionary religious restrictions in favor of their own spiritual development and fulfillment. In this way, seekers will continue to gain more freedom and spiritual agency through the non-traditional mystical practices of their choosing.

The letter from "Veritus" prompts me to explain what I do in a clair-voyant reading and to dispel any apprehension that my work is inspired by evil forces. First, "Veritus" asked if my "mind is different from the rest of ours?" No, I simply put more of it to use than many other Westerners. In our culture we are conditioned to filter out our mystical perceptions and shut down a large portion of our natural conscious functioning. Clairvoyance relies on the use of one's natural higher spiritual centers (6th and 7th chakras) to inquire and receive information directly, not through communication with other spirits, dead or alive. I meditate for 30 minutes before the session to clear my energy, remove distractions, and enter a light trance. I align myself with my own higher conscious-ness and set sacred space. I state my clear intention that the readee and myself are protected by Divine love and that only my readee's highest spiritual good will be served during the session. During the reading, in-formation may be received in the form of images, patterns of energy, or flashes of insight or "knowingness." Many clients have expressed their gratitude through thank you cards and online reviews recognizing how their clairvoyant session helped them resolve problems and find their way forward. Beyond helping clients move from a place of stuckness or despair, I work to inspire them about their own natural psychic gifts. Through meditation and training, they can develop clairvoyance or other psychic functions if they so choose. That with practice, they can strengthen communication with their own soul and even connect with their spirit guides, angels, and God.

The word "veritus" (veritas, feminine form) is Latin for "truth." I do believe that in our earnest seeking, that truth is found and it frees us. We are all naturally curious and want to know what is true. This can be a joy-ful journey that we can travel together with tolerance and good will. To name oneself "Veritus" though, and attack and condemn all clairvoyants based on misinformation is to do a disservice to the truth. Fear-based attacks on mystical and clairvoyant experience simply impede spiritual progress and undermine people's earnest quest for higher consciousness. And higher consciousness is a doorway to communing with God—All That Is— through joyful, direct contact.

Exercise 4
Your Psychic History and Manifesto

I invite you to sit down and write about your personal psychic history since you were a child. Get out your psychic journal and recount all of those psychic experiences you had as a kid and progressing into adulthood. What beliefs were you raised to embrace and did they allow for and validate these psychic experiences? Talk about what happened and how you felt about it at the time. Did you share your psychic experiences with other people? What messages were you given by others about these experiences? Were you validated or told that you were just imagining things or dreaming? That your experience was or wasn't true? Or were you humiliated or punished? Try to be as detailed and comprehensive as possible. Usually starting this exercise will evoke more memories over time that you had forgotten. Keep adding them into your journal so you capture as much of your psychic history as possible.

If you do not recall having psychic experiences, do you remember knowing people or witnessing psychic events in others or in a certain place or situation? Allow yourself to open up these memories without judgment or fear. Just allow it to flow and write about these experiences as you recall them.

Next write about what your intention is now for your own personal psychic development. What abilities do you want to develop or strengthen through meditation, psychic exercises, and regular practice? Create your psychic manifesto! Do you have a knack for a particular kind of psychic ability demonstrated through direct experience? Do you have a psychic history to reclaim for yourself and validate now? Be clear about what you believe you are able to do and what you want to develop in the future.

One thing is for certain: you can never develop and hone a skill if you don't first *believe it is possible*. Remembering your early psychic experiences helps you to get there. Reclaiming them helps you to empower yourself. Stating your intention clearly gives you a direction, a pathway forward on your mystical quest.

Chapter 5

Breaking Through to Wholeness: Freeing the Ego-Bound Self

The ego will endure the worst agonies of neurotic misery rather than consent to one minute of diminishment of its sense of importance.
—Helen Luke

My observation is that most people experience themselves as a mind mobilized by a body that takes them where they want to go to do what they want to do. Upon waking in the morning, we are greeted by those familiar mental messages which then drive the decisions and actions of our day. The range of consciousness is defined, predictable and routine under most circumstances. Each day we take on those activities that we predict will get us what we need and don't question that there could be a broader spectrum of consciousness available to us naturally. Over time, we may begin to feel unsatisfied or sense something is missing and begin to yearn for greater spiritual experience. We may go on a retreat or take up a new meditation practice to help us get in touch with neglected parts of ourselves and seek a deeper range of experience. But what do many realize when they begin a new meditation practice? They can't stop their mind from chattering and mulling over mundane issues of the day. A grocery list has been composed before the new meditator even realizes they had forgotten their plan to focus mindfully only on their breath. This is the most common experience I hear from people embarking on a new meditation journey. After a few weeks of trying unsuccessfully to still their mind, transcend the mental chatter, and experience a stirring of spiritual insight, they give up.

I quote Seth: "Most of my readers are familiar with the term 'muscle bound.' As a species you have grown 'ego bound' instead, held in a spiritual rigidity, with the intuitive portions of the self either denied or distorted beyond any recognition" (Roberts, Seth Speaks 7). We as a species cling to our focus in physical reality. We seem unable to focus our consciousness transcendently even when we try to let go and shift gears. The third chakra, located at the solar plexus, is the seat of the ego. Just as the sixth chakra at the forehead is the seat of clairvoyance and intuitive insight, the third chakra is where we identify who we are and what we need to do to survive and succeed in the physical world. The ego's drive through force of will, a primary function of the third chakra, is indeed very important as it helps us navigate physical reality successfully. We need it to stay safe, obtain food and shelter, and become successful in our worldly endeavors. And indeed, we are an extremely third chakra culture here in the Western world. We are driven by the need not only to survive but achieve towering goals and prove ourselves in the world and to ourselves. The ego is hungry and we are bound to its controlling nature. It will fight our attempt to develop new aspects of our consciousness for fear of losing control. Meditation is fraught; the ego chatters and the distractions discourage us in our spiritual quest. This "ego bound" predicament brings to mind an imaginary boardroom where a meeting of seven members of an organization is taking place. At the table are: an elder with much life experience and wisdom (7th chakra), an intuitive with penetrating insights (6th chakra), a communications specialist (5th chakra), a compassionate community activist (4th chakra), a driven businessman (3rd chakra), a psychotherapist and relationship coach (2nd chakra), and a health and wellness specialist (1st chakra). The whole team brings everything the organization needs to consider the issues at hand from multiple perspectives and make sound, balanced decisions. But the businessman dominates the conversation and cuts anyone off who tries to get a word in edgewise. Meeting after meeting, the businessman—the ego of the organization (3rd chakra)—controls the conversation and blocks input from the others until finally the other six members stop contributing suggestions. This imaginary organization is "ego bound" as Seth would say. And the strategies it would employ are fraught with blind spots, missed insights and opportunities which could have been offered by the other six members. The company's long-term success is weakened because it failed to consider all other perspectives available to it.

In *Seth Speaks*, the imbalance between the inner self and outer ego is covered in-depth. I quote:

> All of your attention is focused in a highly specialized way upon one shining, bright point that you call reality. There are other realities about you, but you ignore their existence, and you blot out all stimuli that come from them. There is a reason for such a trance, as you will discover, but little by little you must wake up. My purpose is to open your inner eyes (Roberts, *Seth Speaks* 28).

These inner levels of perception and experience are operating continuously and simultaneously with the "outer ego" but are largely filtered out from our conscious awareness. We are conditioned to ignore them. But they *do* communicate, albeit below the level of conscious awareness, to coordinate your life and help find new creative approaches to life's challenges. "All necessary information is given to you through these inner channels, and unbelievable inner activities take place before you can so much as lift a finger...This portion of your identity is quite natively clairvoyant and telepathic, so that you are warned of disasters before they occur, whether or not you consciously accept the message..." (Roberts, *Seth Speaks* 9). It's reassuring to know that we do *receive and integrate* this broader range of information and guidance even though it doesn't register consciously. But why filter it out when we can choose to experience it with our full awareness and live within a fascinating multidimensional reality? And wouldn't it satisfy our soul's basic need for mystical experience?

Aldous Huxley, in his 1954 book *The Doors of Perception*, explores the deep-rooted human need for transcendent experience. Almost 70 years later, this book continues to arouse controversy because he openly discusses mind-expanding drugs. Huxley asserts that the need for transcendent experience is found in cultures throughout the world—from indigenous peoples of every region to the urban populations of all modern civilizations. Self-transcendent experience which brings inspiration and a deeper sense of meaning—whether drug induced or not—is propounded by Huxley as a fundamental need of all people no matter their culture. If our religious and our spiritual practices don't satisfy this basic need, then people often turn to its chemical surrogates: alcohol and drugs. From Huxley's perspective, then, the "ego bound" condition we suffer runs counter to human nature and our deep-rooted need for transcendent experience. "To be shaken out of the ruts of ordinary perception, to be shown for a few timeless hours the outer and the inner world, not as they appear to an animal obsessed with survival or to a human being obsessed with words and notions, but as they are apprehended, directly and unconditionally, by Mind at Large—this is an experience of inestimable value to everyone..." (Huxley 73).

I agree with Huxley that human consciousness has a natural range which includes heightened states of awareness beyond our ordinary mental state. To abandon transcendent awareness is to cut ourselves off from a fundamental aspect of our life force and the magnificent range of experience that makes us human. But without hallucinogenic drugs how do we break free of the ego bound trap in which we find ourselves? How might we go about transcending "the ruts of ordinary consciousness" and connect with our own higher mind? I can make a few suggestions which helped me on my own journey.

SUGGESTIONS FOR BRIDGING "THE GREAT DIVIDE"

First, to pursue our mystical nature and begin to develop our psychic abilities, it's important to disengage, little by little, the ego's resistance which so stubbornly raises its head each time we approach the bridge to our inner self. What really helped me when I began this journey was to reassure that part of me (the ego identified self), that what I am doing enhances life practically and makes the ego's job much easier and more successful. The ego no longer must bear the entire burden of solving all of life's problems and controlling everything on its own. Welcoming a team of help from other aspects of myself would relieve a tremendous burden on the ego which has had to "go it alone" most of life. That made a big difference seeing this situation from the ego's perspective; the result of opening to my inner self and "supernormal abilities" translates into a better and more successful physical existence. Seth confirms that the ego needs to know the information is useful to its own physical mission. I quote,

> Each of my readers plays a game in which the egotistical conscious self pretends not to know what the whole self definitely does know. Since the ego is definitely a part of the whole self, then it must necessarily be basically aware of such knowledge. In its intense focus in physical reality, however, it pretends not to know, until it feels able to utilize the information in physical terms (Roberts, *Seth Speaks* 71).

It's very important to approach this conversation with the ego in a way that doesn't diminish its value or threaten to cut it off and demote its good standing. Have a talk with this part of yourself and find out what its concerns are; what is it afraid of? Reassure it you value and appreciate all it does for you in your life. Then be disciplined in setting boundaries with your ego. Create some ground rules, some agreements around allowing expression of the whole self, including the spiritual aspects of your being without interference.

Second, imagine yourself as a psychic person. Go back to the exercise of the previous chapter and see what areas you declare as important for yourself to develop. Maybe you have a knack for a particular kind of psychic function. What can you reaffirm about your known abilities and the abilities you would like to begin developing? Daydream about what it would be like to fully develop those psychic abilities. Claim your psychic nature and believe in it. If you feel self-doubt or fear, sit down and journal about it so you can better understand your beliefs and what you might need to process in order to move forward. Your energy system is wired for psychic sight and connecting with your soul's knowingness. Using your natural psychic abilities is your birthright. But it is unlikely that you will experience success unless you feel it is possible to be that psychic person you want to be. So, own it.

Third, when you begin your meditation or psychic experiments, actively pose your questions. *Ask yourself.* When I was learning how to read in my first clairvoyant training program at Aesclepion, I remember sitting quietly and waiting for information to land in my mind about the readee sitting across from me. My instructor whispered in my ear, "Pose a question. It's what stimulates the information." So, for example, with my inner eye, I could see a grey congestion of energy in the readee's solar plexus. So, "ask yourself" what you would like to know. Silently to myself, I would begin to pose clear questions. Is that grey energy his or does it belong to someone else? Okay, I get it; it is his. What emotional tone does it have? I intuit that it is fear. How long has it been there in his aura? I get it's been there almost one year. And so on. Curiosity and active seeking fuels the process of discovery.

Fourth, when you are learning this in the beginning, I suggest you create a "judgment-free zone." Your ego will invariably jump in and invalidate you. Even if you've negotiated with it, it probably still won't be your greatest cheerleader in this department. In the beginning, it may continue to raise resistance and ridicule your psychic attempts. It's helpful to know how to run interference with your ego's messaging. This is where the boundaries come in—a "judgment-free zone" will give you the permission to keep practicing and developing your psychic skills without the heckling.

In addition, you may think clairvoyance operates in a certain way and have rigid expectations about how you will receive information. Maybe you expect a voice to tell you things plainly, or that you will see a movie clip of the future with details and specific information spelled out clearly. This is rarely the case. Some people see pictures or snapshots, some get a sense of knowing, some see energy and intuitively know what it means, some get symbols, and some may hear a single word or phrase. And your system may be different than any of those I just listed. Everyone is a little different in how their psychic information is delivered to their conscious mind. Explore playfully, with enthusiasm and without judgment. With practice, you will get the hang of your own particular psychic language and gain confidence in your own system.

And fifth, be patient. It takes time to build a muscle that hasn't been used for years. Journal about your psychic wins and also the dreams you have that provide psychic clues and helpful guidance. Keep validating yourself and accept that some days will fall flat. I have had those and know from experience that you don't get good at something by throwing your hands up and walking away when you have an off day. Believe in yourself, keep at it, and success will be yours.

I love this quote from Seth that was delivered during one of Jane Roberts' ESP classes held in the 1970s. It inspires me still today.

> I tell you then...listen to the authority of your psyche – of your being! To listen to the voices that you remember when you were children. The voices that spoke to you as you fell off to sleep. I ask you to recapture the courage and joy and expansion you felt as children – when each new day was a miracle to be explored, and there were no authorities to tell you how to explore it... I ask you only to rediscover your wonder... To look, even at the world that you know, from a different viewpoint, where there are no authorities but the joy and authority of your being; where time is not separated into moments; where you waken each moment as you did when you were a child – each moment a new birth, a new fantastic reality in which you had your place and your part to play; where miracles were your own, and rose from the fantastic joy of your own being. That is what I ask you to do – to recapture those moments that existed before you were educated.[1]

As my ego's resistance continued to diminish, clairvoyant training acquainted me with the other aspects of my being and sparked dialogue between the multiple dimensions of my consciousness. When I awaken in the morning now, I know that I am more than just my ego. Yes, I still hear the constant messaging, framing my day in very physical, pragmatic terms. That's okay. But I now know there is more to me and my life than just my ego. With some training and practice, I began to learn how to access my inner world and reclaim my psychic functioning. I learned how my energy system works and how to drive it. I have the choice to close down my third chakra and quiet the ego so that I may get in touch with

---

1 Excerpt from the Seth Center/New Awareness Network Audio Tape Collection MP3/CD#7– included here with permission. Seth Center Director, Rick Stack, recorded Jane Roberts' ESP classes in the 1970s and was one of her students. Channeled through Roberts, Seth addresses students during an ESP class in Elmira, New York.

spirit and connect with a higher perspective. I will offer several exercises to help you on your journey.

The beautiful thing about this quest is not only that I learned how to perform clairvoyant readings for myself and others, but my entire orientation in life also changed. With this new inner awareness and improved inner communication, I began to experience more subtle urgings and messages from my inner self during the day. Impulses to either seek a specific kind of information or do a particular thing, often synchronistically revealing some answer to a question I had been mulling over. The multi-dimensional parts of my being began working together as a tag team. This is how life is meant to work.

I encourage you to patiently, day by day, break through to wholeness. Invite the inner urgings of your mystical self to whisper in your ear each and every day. Seek your insights playfully and spontaneously. When your ego blocks your efforts, set a boundary with it and try your meditation again for at least five more minutes. When you believe you are a psychic person and embody your transcendent nature, more and more of these experiences will break through into your daily life. Invite them with enthusiasm and anticipation. Be grateful and journal about your successes. This is your life and your time on the planet as your unique self. Embody and enliven the entire spectrum of consciousness that is you. You can own it and use it however you choose. And be patient.

Exercise 5
Have a Conference with Your Ego

In this exercise, you will discover what your ego's concerns are regarding developing your natural psychic abilities. Ask your ego directly what it fears. You may do this as a writing exercise in your psychic journal. Listen patiently and don't judge the things that come up. Note each concern. Keep the dialogue going by posing the question, "And what else are you concerned about?" Be compassionate and patient. Keep going until you have finally exhausted the many resistances that bubble up to the surface. Take a few days to ponder this list of concerns.

Next, brainstorm how these might be addressed and craft some agreements which you also record in your psychic journal. Once again, sit down with your ego for another conference. Read your agreements and feel into whether your ego is satisfied with your solutions. If there are more concerns, notate them and continue to troubleshoot. At the end of this process, you should have a clear set of agreements which define and shape how the various aspects of yourself—both ego and inner spiritual self—can co-exist and support one another.

My main agreement is that my ego may not trespass on the time which is set aside for my meditation and inner explorations. When my mind wanders, I gently redirect it to my spiritual exercises and remind my ego of the many hours I have devoted that day to egorelated activities. Our agreement is about balance. Another important agreement I have is the "judgment-free zone." When I practice psychic exercises, if I hear the ego/critic invalidating my intuitions, those negative messages go straight in the trash chute in the corner of my mind. You can go back over your findings later and decide what was strong and what needs more practice, but from a constructive guidance space, not from "the inner critic" who maligns your endeavors and discourages you from continuing.

Exercise 6
Affirming Your Psychic Nature and Intention

The Power of Affirmations. Review your "psychic manifesto" journaling from the previous chapter. Identify your primary psychic aspirations and goals, and then compose some affirmations that support your progress toward those goals.

For example, you might have said that you remember having psychic experiences as a child but were invalidated for them. You became confused. In your manifesto, you might have identified reclaiming those experiences in your psychic history and validating them for yourself in present time. You also decided that you will move forward and continue to develop these psychic abilities so you may enjoy them as an adult. Your affirmation might say: "I own my lifelong clairvoyant nature and claim these abilities as my truth. Every day I encourage and validate my abilities and they just keep growing stronger every day."

Perhaps create three or four positive statements that tie back to your manifesto or expand upon it. Write the statements out and keep them handy. It's helpful to repeat them every day or choose the one that resonates that particular day. You may find yourself creating new ones as you advance. This helps ground your goals and provide inspiration for your continuing psychic success.

Exercise 7
Swinging on the Golden Thread

*Imagine a golden thread of light running from the infinite cosmos overhead down through your spine and all the way down to the center of the planet. Then imagine a light golden bead of energy about the size of a marble sliding gently along this filament.

*See the golden bead travel upward high over your head and resonate at the high frequency of cosmic energy...feel that frequency in your body.

*Then imagine this bead of golden energy sliding back down, gently through your body and all the way down to the center of the earth. Feel the difference in the earth's energy. Notice this slower, more sedate vibration which is calming and nourishing for the body.

*Then see the golden marble float up again through you and back up to the sky way overhead. It might go higher and higher still on each succeeding cycle.

*Allow this golden bead to deliver these earth and cosmic frequencies into your body as it swings gently up and down through your body and the spectrum of vibrations.

*Open to the truly amazing range of energy frequencies available to you. Continue this for several cycles and feel how these energies nourish you and support your life.

This is fun to do when out walking in nature. It reminds me of playing on a swing set when I was a kid. Traveling up to the top of the arc and feeling weightless, and then swooping back down again to the earth. We usually only experience a narrow band of energy during our daily lives so it's fun and energizing to become reacquainted with the infinite spectrum of energy frequencies we can access.

HOT TIPS

Try writing down a few questions in your psychic journal that you would like your soul to answer for you. Keep them simple and be sure to write them out clearly. Set the intention that the answers will find you at just the right time and in just the right way for you. Expect it. You may receive your answers in a meditation, or a synchronous event, or in a dream. There are so many ways our inner selves deliver messages to our conscious mind from our soul. Begin the dialogue and be respectful of the natural way your inner self communicates information to you. Be patient. You are establishing your new lifestyle and identity as an "intuitive."

PART TWO

Understanding Your Multidimensional Self:
The Human Energy System and How to Drive It

Chapter 6

The Invisible You:
Understanding Your Energy Anatomy

Everything is energy and that's all there is to it.
This is not philosophy. This is physics.
—Albert Einstein

Many books about "alternative healing" and subtle energy systems lay out for the reader diagrams of the aura, chakras, meridians and nadis and discuss their functions. But I thought it would be helpful to drill down a little deeper into some of the evidence for the systems and a framework for understanding the role they play in physical health and the processing of conscious experience. Because the form of clairvoyance I use to help clients is to read the information held in their energy fields so I might determine the origin of dysfunctional patterns, an understanding of the human energy system is vital. Beyond reading yourself and others for the purpose of healing, understanding and embodying your entire multi-dimensional self with joyful awareness is one of life's most profound delights. So, let's create a road map for the invisible you and explore what we know about these systems.

A source for whom I have great respect is the late Richard Gerber, MD, author of *Vibrational Medicine: The #1 Handbook of Subtle-Energy Therapies*. In his book, Gerber does a superb job of explaining the energy fields associated with human body and its functioning from a MD's perspective. He explains how the energy fields interact and support health and in fact, play a central role in every aspect of our lives and functioning.

Western medicine has traditionally held a very Newtonian perspective about the body and health, viewing our physical bodies as the only dimension that exists—that consciousness was only a byproduct of the brain and central nervous system. But neuroscience researchers have never been able to pinpoint the seat of consciousness and the originating source of the will—that essential force which drives the brain's execution of commands. Gerber comments,

> Also, mainstream medicine suffers from an extreme narrow-mindedness in thinking because of its steadfast focus upon the Newtonian worldview of people as sophisticated biological machines. Vibrational healing philosophies have the unique perspective that human beings are more than flesh and blood, proteins, fats and nucleic acids. The body would be a pile of dis-ordered chemicals were it not for the animating life-force that maintains and organizes our molecular substituents into living, breathing, thinking individuals. This life-force is part of the spirit that animates all living creatures. It is the so-called 'ghost in the machine' (Gerber 22).

Gerber posits that the life-force which drives the physical body is the human spirit and that from the spiritual realm the higher dimensional energy systems download directly into the computer hardware we call the brain and body (Gerber 23). These energy systems have been recognized and comprehended by ancient schools of healing around the globe, but our scientists and medical community do not recognize them because they cannot be *observed* and studied through anatomical dissection. This world is invisible and undetectable when approached through our tradi-tional methods of research and observation, not to mention instruments which are not advanced or sensitive enough to detect subtle energy.

But the old Newtonian paradigm of physics must move into the Einsteinian perspective now that we have discovered the properties and actions of energy itself with a more comprehensive understanding and more advanced research instruments. "That greater picture is the extended viewpoint of humans as multidimensional beings of energy. Quantum physics and experiments in high-energy particle physics have shown us that, at the particle level, all matter is really energy. Einstein-ian medicine is a viewpoint that tries to put the Newtonian picture of the bio-machinery into the perspective of dynamic interactive energy sys-tems" (Gerber 24). We might understand the "physical universe" simply as energy vibrating at a lower frequency creating more dense energy patterns. At the quantum level of subatomic particles, all matter is really just "frozen light" (Gerber 69). Let's examine some of the evidence behind the assertion that we humans, and all living organisms, are made up of interacting energy fields.

Gerber explores laser light and the creation of holograms and their significance in understanding a new model of reality—the "holographic universe." A hologram is a three-dimensional picture which forms through *energy interference patterns. The notion that every piece of a system contains within it the essence of the whole springs from the holographic phenomenon* (Gerber 45). Please refer to the appendix at the back of the book for a basic description and visual illustration about how holograms are created for more information.

What is remarkable about holograms is the fact that when a beam of laser light interacts with an object, *it then holds within it a three-dimensional record of that object.* This is not true of incandescent light; only coherent laser light can produce a hologram. What is also fascinating about holographic pictures is that you can cut a little piece of the holographic film which has recorded on it only a tiny piece of the object, and then hold it up to laser light. And guess what you see? Not just the piece that was recorded on that tiny fragment of film, but the whole image of the object photographed! This is because *holograms are energy interference patterns where every piece contains the whole* (Gerber 47).

What does the holographic principle and energy interference patterns have to do with our human energy system? Gerber extends holographic theory to nature and to the body. We know that every cell in the human body contains a copy of the master DNA blueprint. This blueprint has the coded information needed to make an entire body from scratch. This is how cloning works. You can take a single cell from any part of a body and exchange it for the DNA from the same animal's fertilized egg and it will still create a completely identical animal without using normal reproduction processes. This biological fact reflects the holographic principle whereby every piece contains the information of the whole (Gerber 49). We have known this for a long time, but what has always been curious to me is how the original cells from the fertilized egg know which kind of tissue to become and where its appropriate position is in the newly forming body. Gerber provides this theory: "...the spatial organization of the cells is ordered by a complex three-dimensional map of what the finished body is supposed to look like. This map or mold is the function of the bioenergetic field which accompanies the physical body...a holographic energy template that carries coded information for the spatial organization of the fetus..." (Gerber 51). The hypothesis that our physical bodies have a subtle energetic counterpart, a holographic template, is evidenced through some early pioneering research. Harold S Burr, a neuroanatomist at Yale University in the 1940s, studied energy fields around plants and animals. He used a salamander to study these fields and what he discovered was an electrical axis inside the creature extending from its brain and along its spine. He also studied developing seedlings and their electrical fields. He found that the electrical field surrounding the sprout wasn't the shape of the seed but instead the shape of a fully grown adult plant! (Gerber 52)

Gerber cites other early evidence for human energy fields including "electrographic photography" begun by a Russian researcher, Semyon Kirlian, also in the 1940s. "Kirlian photography" created experimental techniques to measure changes in the energy fields of plants and animals. While Burr used a voltmeter to produce data by studying superficial skin measurements, Kirlian studied the same electrical fields using electrography so that the electrical measurements could be translated into visual data and images. Kirlian photography, or early basic electrophotography, is based upon observations of what became called "corona discharge" or the energy fields surrounding living organisms, the "Kirlian aura."

What has been termed "Phantom Leaf Effect" also demonstrates the bioenergetic growth template theory by showing how by cutting off the upper third of a leaf from a living plant and applying electrophotography techniques, you will find photographed the entire intact leaf, not the amputated leaf actually photographed. Gerber suggests that some kind of organized energy field is interacting with the electrons of the corona discharge in the area of the amputated leaf. An energy interference pattern is created forming the image of the whole, intact plant. This, again, demonstrates the holographic nature of the subtle energy body surrounding all living organisms. Termed the "etheric template," these studies suggest that this subtle energy mold has recorded within it all the specifications for the body and guides the cellular growth of the physical structure. It also provides the structural information need-ed to repair the physical body and in the case of a salamander, guides the growth of a new limb in the event the original one was lost. This research illuminates what "the ghost in the machine" might actually be: our energetic "spiritual" counterpart, which precedes and guides our physical form.

This etheric template lies just outside the physical body outside the skin. But what of the other layers of the subtle energy system? The etheric template only makes up the first layer. "The only difference between the etheric body and those higher bodies...is that of frequency characteris-tics" (Gerber 121). The further you travel out from the physical body the higher the frequencies, creating multiple interpenetrating layers of the aura.

Gerber relies on Dr. William Tiller's, model which only defines four auric layers. The late Dr. William Tiller, PhD., was a professor emeritus of materials science and engineering at Stanford University. His book, *Science and Human Transformation: Subtle Energies, Intentionality and Con-sciousness*, explores concepts about subtle energies and how they work in concert with human consciousness. Tiller's model differentiates the auric layers or "bodies" by their purpose and function. Tiller's first auric layer, of course, is the etheric body which we have already discussed. The second layer is the "astral body" responsible for processing our feeling nature. One of the characteristics of the astral body is its mobility and ability to project itself whereby "the transfer of consciousness from the hard-neuronal wiring and fixed time-frame of the physical brain's waking reality into the astral vehicle of consciousness" is not only possible, but common (Gerber 157). The astral body is the interface between our phys-ical experience in temporal reality and the higher mental and spiritual functions located in the mental body (third layer) and the causal body (the fourth and outermost layer). According to Tiller, the mental body is responsible for mental processing spanning from instinctual, intellectual to the spiritual. The outer most auric layer is the causal body and it is the bridge to the soul, the higher spiritual self, and its frequency is high-est of the preceding layers. Because of the "Principle of Nondestructive Coexistence," these layers of energy can interpenetrate one another and coexist without distortion. This principle tells us that matter of varying frequencies can occupy the same place simultaneously, and nondestructively (Gerber 137).

The chakra and energy field model I am familiar with (by way of my experience in clairvoyant readings) are the seven layers of the aura *which are extensions of the seven primary in-body chakras*. Tiller collapses the seven layers down to four based on the primary functions of each within the overall energy system. But they may be further differentiated by the chakras.

All conceptual models agree that the layers interpenetrate one another and are stacked by frequency of vibration. If you were to view them clairvoyantly, they appear much like the light spectrum from slower frequencies of red (lying closest to the body) through to the faster indigo and violet frequencies which are the outermost layers of the aura. Again, the body, or matter, vibrates at the lowest frequency. It should be noted, however, that the auric layers can run, and so display, other frequencies (colors) depending on what that person is processing at the time and their overall mental and emotional condition. When you "read the aura" you will see many different color variations for people depending on the person's situation and their mental/emotional reaction to it.

The following section describes the particular energy system model I use when engaged in a clairvoyant reading or doing a hands-on energy healing session.

THE SEVEN PRIMARY IN-BODY CHAKRAS & AURIC LAYERS

Chakra is a Sanskrit word which means spinning wheel. When viewed clairvoyantly, that is what they resemble: spinning wheels of energy, interpenetrating the physical frame and extending out into the etheric template of the aura, or energy field. "Anatomically, each chakra is associated with a major nerve plexus and endocrine gland. They are situated in a vertical line ascending from the base of the spine to the head" (Gerber 128). I think of this interrelationship in the following way: the chakras—the focal points within a person's overall field of consciousness—registers a particular experience, or stimuli, and instantaneously transmits that data into the physiologic system to activate the appropriate neural and hormonal responses.

You can imagine the spinning chakras and corresponding layer of the aura (which vibrate at the same rate), spreading out around the body for about as far as your arms reach. The whole system of interpenetrating energy fields create the subtle energy "auric egg" surrounding the body you see commonly illustrated in many diagrams. The chakras can also be considered sensitive psychic organs with "extrasensory" non-physical sensing abilities.

Here is an outline of the seven primary in-body chakras, their locations along the spine, their domains of experiential processing, and their extrasensory functions.

First Chakra and Layer One. The first chakra is located at the base of the spine and is responsible for processing and storing information regarding survival, physical health and vitality. Its prime directive is to keep the physical body alive and functioning. The home frequency is red. The first layer of the aura is considered the etheric template and overlays the skin (the layer closest to the body).

Second Chakra and Layer Two. The second chakra is located in the abdominal area, a few inches below the navel. This chakra and the second auric layer make up the emotional body and are responsible for processing information regarding relationships, sexuality, sensuality, boundaries, and working through basic emotions. Female creative energy, mothering and nurturing are all second chakra functions. All emotional issues "in progress" are held in the second layer of the aura. Clairsentience, also known as empathic sensing, or feeling the emotions of others, is a function of the second chakra. The home frequency is orange and the second layer interpenetrates the first layer and spreads out beyond it.

Third Chakra and Layer Three. The third chakra is located at the solar plexus and is the main power pump for the system. It distributes energy through the entire system and can be considered the seat of the ego and the center of the will. Concrete beliefs and identity reside here, as well as feelings of empowerment or disempowerment. Your identity pictures are stored here as well and shape how you perceive yourself and the power you have to influence the world around you. This chakra exerts your will and is concerned with how to carry out your plans and projects. The third chakra is our connection to the astral plane and out-of-body experiences. The home frequency is yellow and the third layer interpenetrates the first two and spreads out beyond them.

Fourth Chakra and Layer Four. This chakra is located at the sternum and is also called the heart chakra. It is the bridge between the spiritual and physical aspects of your nature, and it is the seat of love and compassion. Self-affinity and the bond you have with others, your community, and the Divine is the business of the fourth chakra. The home frequency is green and the fourth layer interpenetrates the first three and spreads out beyond them.

Fifth Chakra and Layer Five. This is the communication center for the entire system. It is your inner communication (inner voice) and your communication with others. Clairaudience (clear hearing) is a fifth chakra function, and so it is the chakra from which you receive spirit communications via mediumship—to hear the messages spoken by discarnate spirits. (Please note that channeling higher beings—like Seth—through *trance mediumship* occurs at the 7th chakra at the top of the head.) The fifth chakra is also instrumental in mobilizing your creative power and, through the power of "the word," speaking your truth. As you will see later, your creative channels move out through the fifth chakra and down through the arms and out the hands (secondary chakras), making your creations manifest. The home frequency is blue and the fifth layer interpenetrates the first four and spreads out beyond them.

Sixth Chakra and Layer Six. The sixth chakra is located at the center of your forehead, also known as the "third eye." Because the chakras interpenetrate the body and extend out through both the front and the back sides of the body, this chakra moves through the pineal gland located in the center of the head. It is responsible for the function of clairvoyance or "clear seeing." It is the chakra most active during a reading and its vibration is one of spiritual neutrality. Group consciousness and abstract intellect are also functions of this chakra and this aspect of the system. The home frequency is deep royal blue/purple and the sixth layer moves through the first five and out beyond them.

Seventh Chakra and Layer Seven. This chakra is located at the top of the head and is therefore called the crown chakra. It is where you receive spiritual insights and information, and really is the spiritual template for your human life. Spiritual information is stored here from this life and other incarnations, and during prayer or meditation, it is in active communication with your inner self, high spirit guides, and God. Your crown chakra is your connection to divine insight and knowing what is true. Trance mediums such as Jane Roberts, for example, use the 7th chakra to "channel" the communications of Seth. The home frequency color is indigo/white, and as the outermost layer of the aura, it is the energy field you show to the world.

Please see "Diagram 2: The Primary In-Body Chakras" on the next page to understand the location and color (frequencies) of each main energy center.

Diagram 2
The Primary In-Body Chakras

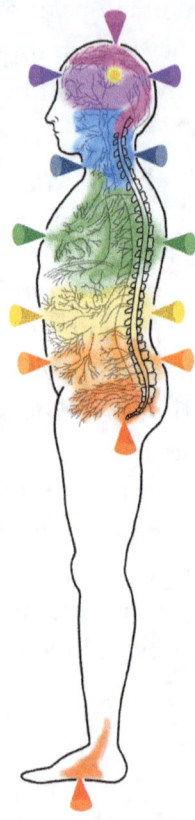

Diagram 2 illustrates the seven primary in-body chakras starting with the first chakra located at the base of the spine (red), the second chakra below the navel (orange), the third chakra at the solar plexus (yellow), the fourth chakra at the heart (green), the fifth chakra at the throat (blue), the sixth chakra at the forehead (royal blue/purple) and the crown chakra at the top of the head (indigo/ white). The chakras feed the appropriate frequencies of energy into the body, infusing the nerve plexuses and endocrine system. The pineal gland (psychic center) located in the center of the head is depicted in our diagram as a point of golden light. Finally, we have included those secondary chakras located on the arches of the feet. They absorb earth energy into the physical system.

—Illustration by Ted Jalbert

There are multiple minor in-body chakras as well. For example, the secondary chakras located in the hands and feet, as we have already discussed. There are even smaller, tertiary chakras located throughout the body at the joints.

In addition to the in-body chakras, there are also five out-of body chakras located above the head and below the feet. The three chakras over the head are called the "creative rings" in the psychic schools. These rings step down and focus the high frequency "spiritual energies" from the causal plane so that they are vibrationally appropriate for each person and therefore easily "metabolized" by their energetic system and body. The creative rings form a portal or beacon through which the causal aspect—the higher self—of each person may engage in 3D reality. Likewise, when a person leaves their body upon death, the rings provide guidance stepping one's consciousness back upward in vibration, returning them to the high frequency causal dimensions.

The last two out-of-body chakras are located below the feet and are related to grounding one's system to the planet. The first chakra is 12 – 24 inches below the feet and is sometimes referred to as the "earth star chakra." It helps balance your entire chakra system by stabilizing your grounding cord so it connects securely to the planet. The earth star chakra helps one to *know their rightful path* and to feel a sense of belonging within the web of life. The last out-of-body chakra is a few feet below the earth star chakra and it serves as a portal to the depths of the earth. This chakra synthesizes the appropriate blend of earth energy to nourish and sustain each person's unique physical system. Through this chakra, this earth energy mix is delivered to the feet chakras where it is absorbed into the body. An athlete uses a different mix of earth energy than an artist or a person working at a desk each day. The out-of-body chakras, then, modulate energy so that it may be used efficiently by each individual to satisfy their particular needs.

THE INTERFACE BETWEEN THE ENERGY SYSTEM AND PHYSICAL BODY

The chakra system steps down energy to the lower frequencies so it may be used to support our physical systems. But the chakras and interacting energy fields of the aura are also responsible for the processing of experiential information—for organizing the action of consciousness. Our chakras also have enhanced perceptual abilities which reach beyond the physical senses. The seven primary in-body chakras drive particular forms of psychic functions such as the clairsentience of the second chakra, astral projection of the third chakra, clairaudience of the fifth chakra, clairvoyance of the six chakra, and high spirit channeling of the seventh chakra.

Conversely, the meridian system—a network of internal energy channels—focuses wholly on maintaining the physiological structure. These in-body energy channels are the basis for the ancient practice of Chinese acupuncture. Energy is carried into the body by way of more than 2,000 acupuncture points located on the skin all over the body. The energy flows in through the superficial points and moves through multiple meridian networks inside the body, each with its own purpose and function to support physical health. Gerber explains,

> Through these meridians passes an invisible nutritive energy known as 'ch'i'. The ch'i energy enters the body through the acupuncture points and flows to deeper organ structures, bringing life-giving nourishment of a subtle energetic nature. The Chinese believe that there are twelve pairs of meridians that are connected to specific organ systems deep within the human structure (Gerber 122).

Research in Korea during the 1960s led by Professor Kim Bong Han studied the acupuncture meridians of rabbits and other animals. By injecting P32 (an isotope of phosphorous) into the acupoints, they then tracked its flow into the tissues. Microautoradiography techniques determined the substance was "actively taken up along a fine duct-like tubule system (approximately 0.5-1.5 microns in diameter) which followed the path of the classical acupuncture meridians" (Gerber 122). The concentration of P32 found in the adjacent tissues was minute. Further, even when it was injected directly into a nearby vein, little to none was found in the meridian system. These findings suggest the meridian system is a separate and independent system from the vascular system. Gerber comments that Western medicine has preferred to think about meridians as imaginary structures and that nerve pathways are instead responsible for acupuncture's therapeutic benefits. But Gerber maintains that instead they are separate systems that work in a "complementary fashion" whereby "each system works in harmony to translate higher energetic events into the cellular patterns of physiology" (Gerber 185). Kim's research also demonstrated that the separate ductile meridian system actively provides energy to the neural networks of the body and the internal organs.

Gerber explains that the chakras are connected to each other and to parts of the physical body by way of even finer energy channels known as "nadis." Because of the location of the highest concentration of these fine energy channels is along the spinal cord, we can visualize the nadis as running primarily along the spine's central nervous system and is responsible for supporting nerve function. "The nadis represent an extensive network of fluid-like energies which parallel the bodily nerves in their abundance" (Gerber 131). He also states that 72,000 nadis channels have been described in the human subtle energy system and they are interwoven with the physical nervous system.

Please refer to Diagram 3 for a visual representation of these aspects of the human energy system.

Diagram 3
The Meridian System, Aura, Secondary Chakras and Grounding Cord

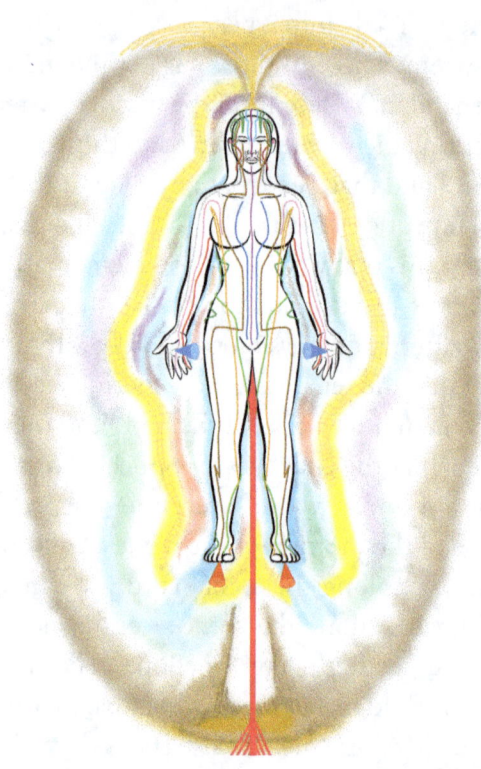

Diagram 3 illustrates the common auric field surrounding the body as it appears clairvoyantly. Notice the layers of the energy field are not perfectly delineated and balanced as you often see in diagrams. They are most commonly irregular and basically stack according to frequency, with red closest to the body and progressing out to the indigo/white outermost (seventh) layer. Our diagram shows the frontal view of the internal meridian channels, as well as the secondary chakras located on the hands and the arches of the feet. The grounding cord, which extends from the first chakra at the base of the spine, connects to the center of the earth and stabilizes the system in the physical plane. Our model is running gold energy at her crown chakra, as in meditation.

—Illustration by Ted Jalbert

WHICH COMES FIRST?
THE CHICKEN OR THE EGG?

William Tiller describes a "ratchet effect" whereby energy inputs from the higher causal level of the energy field must filter down through the mental, astral and etheric levels before they can have their final expression in the physical form. A popular belief is that the body "emanates the aura" or "corona discharge" from its own mass. But to me, that doesn't really make sense given the body's energetic frequency band is the lowest on the scale.

Another viewpoint is just the opposite, and one which Gerber also supports. It is that the energetic system "emanates the body," so to speak. This model posits that there is a stepping-down of energetic frequencies from the highest spiritual frequencies down through the spectrum to the lowest where matter can be held in form or "frozen light." This corresponds with Tiller's "ratcheting effect." The energy ratchets down from higher to lower frequencies, where it then shines through the etheric template, activating holographic blueprint, which then projects its design into form. It creates and animates the three-dimensional physical body. If this is true, it stands Newtonian thinking on its head and challenges us to shift our world view. "It is through the unique connections to our subtle energetic counterparts, via the physical-etheric interface coupled with the chakra system, that there occurs a continuous stream of higher energetic input to our final physical expression and consciousness. These subtle-energy bodies also act as multiple vehicles of containment for our mobile consciousness" (Gerber 197).

Another key property of the energy system is that it is negative-entropic (Gerber 147-8). A thermodynamic rule in the physical universe is that over time, things break down and fall apart. It's known as positive entropy. But "living organisms utilize energy to create increasing levels of order within their physiological systems" (Gerber 302). Our higher energy octaves create and animate our bodies with a negative entropic drive, moving our organism toward greater organization and vitality rather than the disintegrating effect of positive entropy. Well, of course, that is until the time of death when the life-force energy releases from the physical body and the flesh breaks down and returns to dust. It is interesting to note that the body and etheric layer are so enmeshed that when the body dies, the etheric template also dissolves. That's why the phantom leaf effect doesn't work with Kirlian photography when you use a dead leaf; it only works when the leaf is still part of the living plant and only the upper portion is severed (Gerber 302-3). If instead the leaf is cut from the plant and begins to die, then its etheric counterpart has also dissipated and cannot be photographed with electrophotography.

Dr. Tiller proposed that the physical body might just be a simulator of life which we use as a learning tool; a transitory vehicle that we wear to experience and interact with life on the physical plane (Gerber 164). If he is right, this suggests we truly are spiritual beings having a physical experience. We project our consciousness down into the material realm, like a beam of laser light, to create and animate our bodies. Why? I believe we come to earth to learn our lessons through experience, using the gift of our free will. Through our physical explorations and experiential learning, we evolve spiritually—both personally and collectively. Those are my theories, but what do you think?

We have now reviewed the human energy system and in basic terms, how it functions, but what of clairvoyance and inner vision? How does the function of the 6th chakra, the third eye, access information other than through the physical senses? Let's explore how navigating the energy frequencies opens the doors of inner perception.

ACCESSING MULTIDIMENSIONS OF INFORMATION

Gerber suggests that if we are a part of a holographic universe, then we can tap into our own piece of the hologram to access nonlocal information concerning people, places and things existing outside our own physical range. We learn in clairvoyant training that higher dimensions of information can be accessed by shifting our awareness upward in vibration, like taking an elevator up to the higher floors of a building. *"The cosmic hologram is likely to be composed of overlapping energy interference patterns of many different frequencies. Each frequency-specific holographic pattern would carry information of a unique nature relative to the characteristics of that frequency domain"* (Gerber 62).

Remote viewing techniques have demonstrated a person can learn to "zero in on" and describe, often in great detail, geographical locations that were selected randomly by researchers. In the remote viewing experiment, a research participant would travel to the randomly selected location and act as a beacon for the remote viewer. The remote viewers could often describe the geography and key structures and features of the location, even sometimes the weather conditions at the time of the remote viewing experiment. This was studied at the Stanford Research Institute in Palo Alto, CA to explore the original research of Russell Targ and Harold Puthoff, laser and quantum physicists, pioneering the study in this amazing psychic function of remote viewing. Gerber proposes this ability is possible because people can learn to focus their attention inward and tap into their own piece of the cosmic hologram which contains information of the whole, thereby allowing them to zero in on the location targeted by the researchers. They found that everyone could learn to do this. This shows us that all people have access to this level of information storage inherent within the cosmic hologram. This is because we are all a part of the hologram.

The key is in learning to focus your attention and shift into a higher vibratory state, like incoherent light shifting to a laser-like focus, to reach levels of awareness beyond ordinary consciousness. Meditation can be used to discipline this ability which everyone possesses naturally. *"Meditation and other disciplines may condition or 'program' the physical and 'subtle energetic' hardware of our sophisticated nervous system to gain access to higher levels of information. These techniques may allow one to selectively tune the brain/mind receiver to specific frequency bands of energetic input, similar to tuning the station dial on a radio"* (Gerber 65). For those of us trained in the SF Bay Area clairvoyant schools, that is exactly what we do. In this modality, we learn to close down the lower chakras and open up the 6th and 7th chakras located in the head. Then we move our attention up to the 6th chakra—the psychic powerhouse located at the center of the head.

As you practice this and learn to stabilize your attention at these higher frequencies for longer and longer periods of time—new worlds of energy and information are revealed. The hologram contains and reflects *all that is.* We simply need to learn how to access it by tuning our psychic radio dials to these higher frequencies.

In the following chapters, we will explore these techniques in detail and give exercises for you to begin developing your ability to access the clairvoyant dimensions of energy and information. But before we jump ahead, I have provided a guided meditation; a tour of your chakras and energy field so you can begin to sense each level and the corresponding qualities of the "invisible you."

I suggest making notes in your psychic journal about your experience doing this energy system meditation. It's also great to revisit this energy exploration multiple times and try it at different times of the day. You may find you are more sensitive in the morning or in the still, late hours of the night. That will give you a clue to when your inner vision is naturally at its sharpest.

Exercise 8
Guided Tour of Your Chakras and Energy Field

*Close your eyes and take a few deep breaths. Relax and turn your awareness inward. Notice the temperature of the air on your skin and the gentle movements of your breathing. Notice the feeling of your feet on the ground and your body resting comfortably in your chair. Be present in the moment.

1st Chakra: Now notice the base of your spine and imagine a warm red glow about the size of an orange there. This is your first chakra and it is concerned with keeping your body alive and healthy. This is also the chakra from which you ground to the planet. Feel the energy here and notice any images that come to mind. It is the slowest vibration of all the primary in-body chakras and closest to the earth's frequency. Move your awareness gently outward from the center of this chakra and into the first layer of your aura closest to your body. This is the etheric template. Notice any colors, images, symbols or feelings you sense here in this first layer. Make a mental note and then gently move back into your first chakra. Thank it for supporting your physical body, health and vitality.

2nd Chakra: Next, move your awareness up from the base of your spine to your abdomen, a few inches below your belly button. See a warm ball of orange energy here, its vibration is a little faster than the first chakra. This chakra is concerned with emotions, relationships, and sexuality. Notice any impressions you get as your awareness rests in the second chakra; notice its vibration and any feelings that might be processing here. Have you been experiencing a particular emotion lately or working through a relationship issue? With neutrality, acknowledge this work and thank this chakra for its expertise in processing your feeling nature. Gently project your awareness out through that first layer closest to the body and just beyond it into the second layer of your aura. Its "home vibration" is an orange color. Notice any feelings you may be processing here. Just say hello to these and make a mental note of any information that comes to you. Now move back inward to the center of the second chakra.

3rd Chakra: Now gently move up again, this time to your solar plexus where your stomach is located. See a warm glow of yellow energy here. The 3rd chakra is concerned with your will, action, identity, and personal power. It is the seat of the "ego" and where most of us operate during our busy day. Notice the vibration here; it's faster than the 1st and 2nd chakras. Check in and see if it feels tight here or maybe you're holding your breath. Take a few cleansing breaths and release any tension held here as you exhale.

This chakra is your main power pump and is responsible for distributing energy throughout the whole system. Now gently venture outward from the 3rd chakra and through the first and second layers of your aura until you reach the third layer. Notice the quality of energy here and what comes to you as you tune in to this layer. Do you notice images or symbols or information about what you are focused on in your life now? Make a mental note and just sit with the energy here for a minute and breathe. When you're ready, move back into the center of your 3rd chakra at your solar plexus.

4th Chakra: Now move your awareness even higher to your heart area in your chest, just below your clavicle bones. See a soft spring green light glowing here. This chakra's domain is the unifying power of love and compassion. It is also the bridge between our spiritual and physical experience. Notice any impressions you get as your awareness rests lightly in the soft green 4th chakra. What symbols or images come to you about the power you hold here in your heart chakra? When you're ready, move outward into your aura through the first three inter-penetrating layers and into the fourth layer. What do you sense? Thank it for its loving action in your life and then return inward to the center of the fourth chakra.

5th Chakra: Now allow your attention to move up even higher to the base of your throat. This is the 5th chakra and its home vibration is blue. This vibration is even faster than the first four chakras and its business is communication. This chakra is a creative powerhouse and its expression fuels your manifestation of new endeavors. Notice any impressions you get as your awareness explores the 5th chakra at your throat. Now move gently outward through the first four layers of your aura and into the fifth layer which is a higher frequency than the preceding four layers. Sit in this blue energy and sense into what is here. What images, messages or symbols show themselves to you? This layer holds and processes issues regarding communication. Now move gently back into the center of your throat chakra. Acknowledge the creative force it is in your life.

6th Chakra: Draw your attention up to your forehead just above your eyebrows. The 6th chakra is a primary spiritual chakra; it is the seat of your clairvoyance. It is sometimes referred to as the 3rd eye. It vibrates at a deep cobalt blue/royal purple vibration that is faster than the lower five chakras. The pineal gland in the center of the head is the psychic center and where clairvoyance operates. The energy here is a neutral spiritual vibration. Do you notice any messages or images here? Ask yourself what symbol you can use to acknowledge and activate this chakra? Then when you're ready, move out from this chakra through the first five layers of your aura and into the 6th layer. Feel how different the energy is here. Does it remind you of anything? What symbols or images do you notice?

Make a note of what you sense here and then gently withdraw back to the center of the 6th chakra at the center of your head.

Seventh Chakra: Finally, bring your attention to the very top of your head. The crown chakra vibrates at indigo/white and is the fastest vibration of all the in-body chakras. It is where you connect with your soul self, and where you *know* what is true. It is the source of your wisdom and the portal to other dimensions and non-physical realities. Notice any messages or impressions you get as you rest your focus on this chakra at the top of your head. What does the energy feel like here? What images, symbols or messages do you notice? Acknowledge the expansive power of your seventh chakra.

*Spend a couple of minutes here and then move outward through the first six layers of your aura and into the seventh layer. It is the outside layer of the aura and the one you show to the world. What do you notice about this layer and the qualities of energy here? Sense into it and make note of what you discover here. Then gently move back into your crown chakra. Thank it for its wisdom and guidance in your life.

*Gently glide back down to the third chakra at your solar plexus. Take a few deep breaths and thank your energy system for its support and facility in navigating the energetic universe and creating your life. Gently open your eyes.

My CT instructor at Aesclepion proposed that the chakras store finished information, your truth, while the aura really reflects what is still "in progress." When we "read the aura" we are exploring those questions or issues which are still in progress or in some cases stuck and causing a dysfunctional pattern or condition. He believed that when a person finally breaks through to a true understanding about a particular issue or condition—has that ah-ha moment—the energy imprint of the "problem"

held in the aura dissolves and the truth becomes stored in the associated chakra. In addition, we learn that each frequency level houses a specific kind of information, and it is our job to tune into, or match, that vibration to access that domain of information. The next chapter will teach you to tune-in clairvoyantly, and therefore access multiple dimensions of information.

Chapter 7

Preparing for Clairvoyant Work & How to "Run Your Energy"

In actuality, by shifting one's frequency focus, one may be shift-
ing his/her consciousness from the viewing perspective of the
physical up to the astral, mental, causal and higher energetic
levels which are all a part of our energetic expression.
—Richard Gerber, MD Vibrational Medicine

There are many different kinds of psychic functioning, as touched on earlier in this book. Reading the energy field clairvoyantly for the purpose of identifying and shifting unresolved issues and blocks is my particular form of clairvoyance. That will be the primary emphasis for this chapter. By practicing the energy meditations and exercises already presented in this book, you will become more energy aware and sensitive so that multiple forms of psychic functioning may begin blossoming naturally.

As many times as you can, I encourage you to practice the grounding exercise, the "Clearing Your Psychic Center" exercise, the "Swinging on the Golden Thread" exercise, and the energy field tour. The golden thread exercise helps you become more flexible in the range of energy levels you can access and feel in your body. The chakra tour helps you to learn the particular tone and qualities of each chakra and associated layer so that navigating your energy field and the fields of others is much less abstract and mysterious. As you become more proficient in these techniques, moving into "reading" and clearing blocks in the aura will be much easier. By learning to occupy each chakra with your attention you will learn more about the gifts of a particular chakra and how to harness each. This preliminary practice is time well spent on your clairvoyant journey and really for any other form of psychic work you want to develop.

"READING" THE AURA

Pictures—The Language of the Soul

When I talk about reading the aura, you may wonder what I am looking at exactly. In clairvoyant training we learn to see spiritual "pictures" held in the energy field. The aura is packed with pictures and they vibrate at particular frequencies and contain the emotional charge related to the content represented by the images. In their book, *Basic Psychic Development*, John Friedlander and Gloria Hemsher describe spiritual pictures in the following way:

Bound-up psychic energy blocks, frozen in time, are called 'pictures.' As you become clairvoyant, you can often see actual images of unprocessed experiences. Every experience is momentarily created as a picture. Ideally, when each experience is over, the experience is processed and resolved unconsciously by the person. When the experience is processed, the memory is stored in psychic memory banks and the energy held in the picture of the experience becomes free and available very rapidly. When the experience isn't fully processed or resolved, however, the energy stays frozen and unavailable. A little bit of you gets locked into the past. A block is formed which disrupts the energy flowing through your aura, like cholesterol deposits disrupt the healthy flow of blood in the physical body (Friedlander & Hemsher 35).

These pictures provide a wealth of information about a person's spiritual history, unresolved thought patterns, and habitual modes of operating. Pictures can originate from this life or other lifetimes and are made up of unresolved experiences as well as symbolic representations of false beliefs (one's own and those adopted from others). In tapping this information, we may uncover areas of unresolved trauma, confusion, fear and resistance, or programming related to past experiences. When a client shares with me the particular area with which they are struggling, I see, clairvoyantly, a constellation of energy light up in their aura which are the pictures immediately stimulated by their talking about them. They may represent a new problem, and so be composed of only a single or small collection of pictures, or they may be numerous older, longer-held pictures, even from multiple lifetimes. The pictures will stack according to like content and emotional charge and be held in the appropriate layer of the aura depending on the category of unresolved experience it is. This is the law of attraction.

Like Attracts Like

So why do the energetic pictures stack together in bundles? The reason is that they have a magnetic quality—*like attracts like* on the energetic level. Pictures are stacked together when they are of like content and emotional charge or, in other words, they arrange themselves at the same frequency level because of their resonant magnetic charge.

When a person has a repeating experience and continues to think about it in the same erroneous thought loop, they will add a new picture to the stack which builds up into what we call a "thoughtform." They are stored in the layer of the aura with the same frequency characteristics as the image itself; so physical fears would be held in the first layer of the aura, and emotional blocks and negative relationship beliefs would be held in the second layer, and so on. This is the law of attraction, and the aura is brimming with pictures, energy and information that are stored in discrete stacks of "like" categories. Richard Gerber explores this phenomenon in Chapter Four of his book. I quote: "Certain thoughts may actually be charged with subtle energetic substance and exist (unconsciously) as thoughtforms in the energetic fields of their creators. These thoughtforms can frequently be seen by clairvoyant individuals who are very sensitive to higher energetic phenomena" (Gerber 151). He proceeds to say that these thoughtforms have magnetic qualities which attract "other substances that are in harmony with it."

> It is not the type of magnetism that attracts iron filings, of course, but it is most definitely a species of magnetism... Experimenters will eventually find that emotions must be dealt with both as highly magnetic non-physical matter and as an aspect of consciousness. The difficulty in treating many emotional illnesses

stems, in part, from the fact that the emotions which cause these problems tend to be magnetically responsive to a kind of astral matter which easily 'glues' itself both to our own feelings and to more of its own kind. The magnetic action makes it very difficult to get rid of the 'bad' astral matter—and the emotional problem (Gerber 152).

A person trained in reading these pictures clairvoyantly can also dig down through the stack of pictures to the bottom-most, original experience which set the issue in motion—identifying the origin of the unprocessed experience or emotional block. What these unresolved pictures have in common is that they contain information that does not match *the person's own vibration of truth and so they cannot be fully integrated and stored in the energy system as complete;* they are discordant vibrations which must be reconciled. Often, these pictures can be tracked back to past lives, and even a series of lifetimes where the individual has been working on comprehending and mastering a particular karmic lesson. (I think of karma as a *basic mistake in understanding* which can lead to misguided behaviors and unproductive patterns.) Whether or not the picture is karmic or a new unresolved experience from this lifetime, it needs to be illuminated and reconciled. The mistaken belief and related faulty thinking needs to be rejected and released so they may return to their own individual vibration of truth and alignment with their soul. Here the readee can have that a-ha moment and release the entire stack of images together with the "frozen in time experience" and false belief. This is called "**blowing a picture**." Only then may the frozen energy be freed back into present time and a new more productive understanding be adopted which leads the person in a more fulfilling direction. In so doing, they move out of discord and back into spiritual grace.

The skill of the clairvoyant is not just seeing and reporting the pictures held in the readee's space. It is also holding space for the readee so that, from the perspective of present time, they can be in touch with this old part of themselves that became frozen in the past, and from "the now," they may recognize the inherent weakness of the old false belief and let it go. By "**blowing the picture**" in this way, they are resolving the past experience and updating the associated beliefs. Presuming to know how they need to change and direct them to a new belief is not only faulty thinking on the reader's part, but it can also rob the readee of a valuable opportunity. It's important to trust that people implicitly know their truth and what their next step is. A good reader will lead the readee to the pictures and even back to the originating unresolved experience so that they may have that epiphany for themselves and release the pictures through their own reorientation in thinking.

The same is true for exploring your own unresolved experiences held in your aura. Tread gently and give yourself space. Pictures can be charged and painful so the importance of being gentle and compassionate is paramount. Strong-arming yourself into a contrived positive thought pattern doesn't work—*You can only maintain a positive way of thinking over time if you really believe your new thoughts to be true.* You can only arrive at what you believe to be true by exploring your current set of beliefs honestly and without censorship. Truth arrives on your doorstep (or emerges from your core wisdom) and allows a fundamental shift in perspective and one that "holds" over time. A new viewpoint is born, a perspective which is in harmony with your spiritual truth.

Let's explore the neutral spiritual vibration of high gold which makes this kind of sensitive exploration possible. This gold **"cosmic or universal energy"** moves our awareness up into the higher spiritual frequencies and domains of information. Gold cosmic energy is a neutral vibration and therefore effective at removing the emotional charge connected with energetic pictures. This kind of psychic exploration and transformation calls on us to set the energy for clarity and neutrality to support ourselves and the readee.

Running Cosmic Energy and Setting Your Crown Chakra at Gold

So far, we have practiced grounding our energy to the earth and drawing in earth energy through our feet; clearing the center of our heads and activating the psychic center; and traveling through the chakras and aura to become acquainted with our subtle system. Now we are going to draw in high spiritual vibrations through our crown chakra, called cosmic or universal energy. This helps us to raise our vibration and balance our system between the lower earth vibrations and the higher spiritual frequencies. The cosmic energy comes down from high above us (remember the upper arc of the golden thread exercise) and enters into our crown chakra at the top of our heads. We may alternatively choose to visualize a big warm golden sun over our heads which pours the cosmic energy into our crown—either visualization is fine. The gold energy then flows down your back to the first chakra where it mixes with the earth energy which has been drawn in by the chakras on the arches of your feet. Though there are many vibrations of cosmic energy available, we prefer to use a soft, golden color because it is neutral, calming and works well to raise our vibration and stabilize our psychic sight. To access spiritual information in a reading, we must raise our vibration and move out of the lower chakras and up into the spiritual centers in the head. The reason we don't use white in this exercise is it can be too high a vibration for our body so we can get knocked out of our physical body and into a dissociated state. Clairvoyant programs teach us to remain grounded in our bodies while simultaneously raising our vibration so we can reach higher frequency domains and levels of information.

This practice of running gold cosmic energy pulls the entire process together and will enable you to balance your energy and clear your system naturally. The gold energy comes down gently into your crown, runs down either side of your spine on the backside of your body, mixes with the earth energy in your 1st chakra at the base of your spine, and then travels up the front of your body to the 3rd chakra at your solar plexus—the main energy distribution center. From there, the mix of cosmic and earth energy will distribute throughout your entire system in the proper proportions.

The following exercise will guide you in this procedure. You may feel dizzy as you first begin to work with the high frequencies of cosmic energy, so track how your body feels as you go. You may bend forward in your chair and touch the ground with both hands, allowing your head to bend forward over your knees to allow a discharge of excess energy from your crown chakra. That helps you to reset automatically so that your system isn't overwhelmed by unfamiliar high frequency vibrations.

Exercise 9
Drawing in Cosmic Gold Energy at Your Crown

*Close your eyes and take a few deep, cleansing breaths. Turn your attention inward. Feel your feet on the ground and notice your grounding cord releasing old energy down to the center of the planet. Visualize the sedate, calming earth energy replenishing you through your feet chakras. Say hello to your chakras and gently float your attention up to the center of your head in the sixth chakra.

*Now from the center of your head, imagine a gentle stream of soft, gold, cosmic energy showering down from the heavens and gently entering your crown chakra. This is a much higher frequency than the sedate earth energy you receive through your feet. This high gold energy is neutral and helps you understand your experience and receive insights from your inner self, the spiritual aspect of your nature. Just explore this energy and see if you get any impressions or if it makes your body feel different in any way.

*Now imagine the gold energy flowing gently into your body from your crown chakra and down either side of your spine to your first chakra. See the gold mixing with the warm, red earth energy there in the first chakra. Then visualize this mix moving back up the front of your body through the second chakra and up to the 3rd chakra at your solar plexus. (It moves in a single stream upwards, rather than in a branched stream down your back as it did earlier.)

*From there, the 3rd chakra distributes it according to the appropriate mix just right for your system. This mix of energy infuses your entire system in just the right proportions and helps your body/ego to rest while your mind/spirit shifts gears into the higher frequencies.

*Now just relax and notice any changes in your body sensations and thoughts. Your chakras will modulate how much gold you receive through your crown and how much earth energy you receive through your feet. Just the right mixture for you will be maintained for optimal functioning.

*Allow yourself to float in the gold energy at your crown and in your sixth chakra. Bathe yourself in the warmth of this high spiritual vibration. Say hello to your soul.

*When you feel ready, take a deep breath and lean forward. Hang your head over your knees and touch the ground with both hands. That will help you to release excess energy and rebalance so that you do not get dizzy. Gently, return to the outer world. Get up and walk around to help reset your system. Perhaps write about your experience in your psychic journal.

Our systems often run anxiety, fear, pain and "hurry-up" energy for large portions of our day, straining our bodies and wearing us out. The neutral, calming energies of the earth and the cosmos allow us to rest and take a break. This is deeply restorative and a healthy practice overall. Running this energy through your energetic space helps to maintain neutrality during the day. Neutrality doesn't mean not feeling, it means not judging your feelings. It provides some space between you and your experience so you can observe the situation from a fresh perspective.

Gold cosmic energy may also be used to help resolve conflicts with others or reset a bad mood. By seating yourself in the center of your head and breathing in golden cosmic energy through your crown, you can calm down and gently shift gears into a more neutral perspective. Simply sit down, ground yourself, and breathe deeply and completely, exhaling the tension and conflict and inhaling more gold which will circulate naturally through your system. You may even send the gold vibration to the area of your body you feel registering the conflict or upset. Exhale the unwanted energy through your breath or down your grounding and breathe in more golden light through your crown. When you feel better, bend forward and touch the ground to release any excess energy.

Creating Your Own Psychic Studio

When I first began clairvoyant training, I wanted to have a safe and comfortable inner space from which I did my readings. I created a psychic studio in the center of my head which I imagined as a comfy round room with a big open window gazing out at the readee. My studio was composed of soft silk fabric walls made up in dusty rose and peach tones and stocked with an ample supply of silk pillows. (I'll date myself by mentioning it's similar to the inside of the *I Dream of Jeannie* magic bottle.) Overhead was a skylight with warm yellow sunshine streaming in to illuminate my clairvoyant activities. Then when I prepared myself for a reading by running and clearing my energy and moving up to my sixth chakra, I had an imaginary room I could move my attention into that was familiar and pleasant.

You may get creative and imagine a room of your own which you travel up to for this work. It helped me to feel safe and relaxed which aided my ability to focus clairvoyantly and stabilize myself in this frequency dimension. This is a personal choice, so if it feels unnecessary or too whimsical for your taste, you can skip this and move on.

Using Roses to Transform Energy

The image of the rose is used extensively in our form of clairvoyance because universally, it is a neutral image that helps to buffer emotions and drain off the emotional charge. We may use roses to attract unwanted energy or pictures out of our energy field and then transform it by bursting the rose into gold dust. This is an effective technique to remove old or foreign energy from our (or someone else's) space or in the process of blowing pictures. Some new readers are concerned it is a violent act to burst, or blow-up a rose, but it is simply a way to recycle energy and transform it so it no longer blocks you. We also use roses during a reading to help neutralize content because the image reduces the emotional charge and makes the information easier to read for the clairvoyant, and therefore easier to hear for the readee.

In the following section, I am going to acquaint you with the various uses of the rose to help clean the energy system, blow pictures, create separation between your energy field and that of others, and to exercise your 6th chakra through repeated visualizations involving creating and destroying roses. Let's first build our visualization skills by creating and destroying roses.

Building Your Visualization Abilities

A large part of clairvoyance is building the ability to see images with your inner eye so that you can read them. In clairvoyant training we call the pineal gland the "picture-maker" because it generates the images you experience during dreaming at night as well as the pictures you are able to see clairvoyantly in a reading. This exercise is very simple and will build your "picture-making muscle" so that seeing images clairvoyantly becomes easier and easier. If you don't consider yourself a visual person, this will help you develop the ability. The other benefit of this exercise is the release of energy. If you're having a rough day, for example, by simply grounding yourself and creating and destroying roses, you will effectively release unwanted energy from your system so you can return to a state of calm.

Exercise 10
Creating and Destroying Roses

*Sit down and relax in your chair with your feet flat on the ground. Take a few deep breaths. Just close your eyes, relax and turn your awareness inward.

*Check in with your grounding cord and notice if it is still connected to the base of your spine and running all the way down to the center of the planet. If it isn't or you aren't sure, create a new grounding cord. See the chakras on the arches of your feet open and draw in fresh new earth energy, replenishing your system.

*Now see a big golden sun hovering above your head and allow it to pour its soft golden light in through your crown chakra. Rather than directing it this time, allow the light to move freely through your aura, chakras and body all the way from your head down to your toes. Say hello to this neutral gold and notice how your body feels when you call it in.

*Draw your attention up to your sixth chakra at your forehead and allow it to pull back to the center of your head (about as far back as your ears). Move the cosmic gold energy through your sixth chakra, giving it a little clean-out.

*Now visualize a rose out in front of you maybe four feet (outside your aura) and at about eye level. Imagine it to be any size and color you like. Notice its shape and the color of the petals; notice each aspect of your rose. Fully register this image in as much detail as you can. Take a minute or two focusing on this.

*Next, burst the rose into gold dust or see it dissolve to golden dust if you prefer. Check in with your body and notice if you feel a shift after destroying the rose.

94

*Create a new and different rose and do the same thing. Notice every detail and take in its qualities so you really *see it* with your inner eye. Examine its various aspects...color of petals, if there is dew on them, how open is the blossom, is there sunlight shining on it? Then when you feel finished, destroy the rose once again.

*Do this multiple times. You may feel some pressure at your forehead as you do this exercise. This is normal. You're giving your picture-making "muscles" a workout! When you are finished, gently bring your attention back to the room and open your eyes. You can rebalance your energy by leaning forward and touching the ground, letting your head dangle for a moment. Thank yourself for taking the time to develop your visualization skills. This will help you to see more clearly and confidently with your inner senses.

With practice, you can learn to create and destroy roses rapidly. It's a great tool for building your ability to visualize images as well as release unwanted energy from your space. As always, it's great to note down any experiences you had in your psychic journal so you can track your progress with these exercises.

Navigating, Cleaning and Resetting the Chakras

Practicing the chakra and energy field tour helps to familiarize you with this system on a personal basis. It's one thing to read about the chakras and another thing to experience them and work consciously with their functioning. When we learn to read clairvoyantly, we are taught the importance of taking care of our energy system and doing regular "maintenance." By learning to clean and reset the chakras, you can experience a shift in consciousness and move from one level to another. I talked about various dimensions of information sitting at the different frequencies of the energy field. When you shut down the lower chakras involved in managing your temporal reality and then float up to the sixth chakra and open it up much wider, you are tuning your radio dial to the world of spiritual information, energy and the auric pictures.

The following exercise will help you to run your energy in the most comprehensive format, clean out each chakra with roses, and then reset the chakras by opening or closing them to a particular percentage. You can imagine the spinning chakras from the front view. From the side they appear to be cones of energy, but viewing them head-on, they look like circles. By enlarging the circles or shrinking them down visually, you can reset them in a way that supports spiritual sight and knowingness and moving at will between the various energy domains. This is like watching the iris of an eye dilate and undilate, or the lens of a (non-digital) camera opening and closing. This is the main preparation we do before a reading. Because you have learned parts of the system of "running your energy" step by step, this final exercise will bring the whole system together for you. As with all of the psychic exercises in this book, I suggest you record this exercise so you can follow it as a guided meditation.

Exercise 11
"Running Your Energy" and Resetting the Chakras

*Sit comfortably in your chair with your feet flat on the ground. Rest your hands in your lap and close your eyes. Breathe restfully, relax, and turn your awareness inward.

*Create a new grounding cord by spinning a soft green ball of energy at the base of your spine and ask it to attract and absorb energy you're ready to let go of. Then drop the ball and see it travel to the center of the planet and connect there. Notice tension and old energy releasing down your grounding cord from your energy field. Check your feet chakras and see them open, inviting in soothing, fresh earth energy. See the energy move up your legs, and this time, allow it to flow back down into your pelvis, filling that first chakra at the base of your spine. Any excess energy flows back down your grounding cord.

*Now see a soft beam of golden cosmic light travel gently down from the heavens and flow into your crown chakra at the top of your head. Let the cosmic energy circulate down your back on either side of your spine to the first chakra where it blends with the earth energy there.

*Gently breathe the mix up the front of your body to the second chakra (two inches below your navel) and see it flow around this emotional center, giving it a clean-out. This energy nourishes and relaxes this chakra so it can take a "drama break." Old, stagnant energy will release naturally down your grounding cord.

*Breathe deeply and move the energy further up your front body to your solar plexus, the 3rd chakra, and again allow it to circulate and fill up this chakra with fresh energy, giving it a little tune-up. Again, see congested energy drop down your grounding cord and release.

*Again, visualize the energy moving up higher to your heart chakra at the center of your chest. Give this chakra a good healing with this calming energy. See it flow around and heal this sensitive chakra of love and compassion.

*Breathe and see the energy move up to your 5th chakra at the throat and flow around this energy center, replenishing it with fresh, neutral energy. From here, see half of the energy branch out and travel down both arms and out the hand chakras (secondary chakras) located on your palms.

These hand chakras are healers and creators. They can supply energy to yourself or others through hands-on healing and also serve as creative channels through which your creations flow out into the world.

*Now see the remaining 50% of the energy at the throat chakra move up to the center of your head in the 6th chakra and replenish it with fresh energy. See it flow around and clear your psychic center.

*Finally, see the energy mix move up to your crown chakra and fountain back out into your aura. You are now officially "running your energy!"

*From the center of your head, place your attention back on your grounding but stay seated in the 6th chakra. Notice your grounding from your psychic center and continue to see old energy gently moving down the grounding cord to the center of the planet. Your system is continually replenished by earth and cosmic energy flowing in your feet and crown chakra.

*Remain in the center of your head and set your crown chakra at gold. Just see a warm golden light glowing there at the top of your head which will set and stabilize your energy at the vibration of truth and neutrality. Relax for a few minutes and notice how you feel.

*Create a soft rose blossom of any color and imagine it to be the size of a grapefruit. Swish this soft fluffy rose blossom through your energy field and gently *vacuum up any remaining tension or congested energy*. Watch it get absorbed into the rose. Play with moving the rose around the front and backs of the chakras and set your intention that the rose gently vacuums out any congested energy that you are ready to release. Clean out your entire field and your body too. If you have tension or pain in your body, clean it out with this **vacuum rose**. When you are finished, move the rose out of your energy field about four or five feet. Now destroy the rose to release and recycle that energy.

*Visualize the 7th chakra from above. Visualize a circle maybe the size of a tangerine. Imagine what it looks like open to 100% and then using that frame of reference, close it down to about 80%. Don't get stuck on what exactly that should look like. Simply visualize the approximation of 80% and say, "my 7th is set at 80%." Then move on.

*Do the same for the 6th chakra. This time see the chakra from the front since it is horizontally oriented (rather than the crown chakra which points straight up). Hypothesize what it would look like at 100% open, then set it to 80% also.

*Do the same for the 5th chakra at your throat. Set it to 80%.

*View your 4th chakra from the front and reset it to 60%.

*View your third chakra at your solar plexus. Close it down to 60%.

*See your 2nd chakra, a few inches below your naval, and close it down to 10%.

*Your first chakra at the base of your spine should also be closed down to 10%. This shifts your energy out of the lower temporal frequencies and up into the spiritual portions of your field so it can activate your clairvoyant function. Your lower chakras get some time off.

*Sit in the center of your head, your psychic studio, and become familiar with how these adjusted settings feel. With time and practice, you will feel confident in your ability to set your chakras up for meditation or clairvoyance quite quickly through your intention and simply stating the setting percentages.

*Create a **"separation rose"** out in front of you about four feet. See it hover there, maybe the size of a soccer ball. This rose will separate your energy from other people and the environment. Ask it to absorb energy which is not yours so that it can't enter your energy field. At the end of the day, you can destroy the rose. If you have a rough day, you can create and destroy multiple roses throughout the day.

*You may rest here for a few minutes and just run your energy and notice thoughts, impressions or creative insights. Or simply breathe and just *be*.

*When you are ready, gently open your eyes and bend forward, touch the ground, and dump any excess energy from your crown chakra. Get up and walk around a bit. Your chakras will automatically reset to "regular" mode.

*You have just learned the system of "running your energy" and entering into a light trance for meditation or clairvoyant work. Congratulations!

This is the main meditation system for running your energy and shifting to higher frequency domains for clairvoyant work. As you begin practicing, try to be playful and not too serious. If something feels hard to accomplish, don't go into effort. Trying too hard will only activate that third chakra and get the ego involved. Assume by visualizing each part of the exercise and setting your intention for each step, it will happen automatically. This is not a time for perfectionism, so be playful instead and see what you discover. *It will work* and you will become more comfortable and confident as you practice this multiple times. Once you have memorized this system, it will only take about 20 minutes to get set up. Then you can spend 30 minutes or more exploring your questions clairvoyantly, meditating, praying, or doing breathwork. As usual, keep some notes of your experiences in your psychic journal so you can track your progress in this foundational exercise.

HOT TIPS

The **"separation rose"** described in the Exercise 11, is an effective tool that creates separation between your energetic space and that of others and your environment. It's always good to place a separation rose just outside the front of your aura when you're going out into public—especially densely populated locations like airports, parties, events, mass transit vehicles, etc. If you notice someone staring at you and you can feel their energy intruding on your space, put out a new separation rose between your body and their line of sight. I find the person looks away immediately, even if I never once glanced at them. The rose interrupts the energy beam of their attention and absorbs it for you so it can't bombard your space. You may create and destroy many separation roses during the course of your day, or simply use one and ask it to destroy itself at night when you are at home or going to bed. Do what feels right for you on that particular day. By using this very effective psychic tool regularly you may enjoy your energy autonomy and feel safe, serene, and far less encumbered by environmental distractions.

Chapter 8

Beginning to Read Clairvoyantly—
Tools, Techniques & Spiritual Healing

*Jesus said, 'Recognize what is in your sight, and that which is
hidden from you will become plain to you. For there
is nothing hidden which will not become manifest.'*
—Non-Canonical Gospel of Thomas, Verse 5
(Cameron 25)

Now that you've become versed in the theory behind clairvoyance, learned how the human energy system functions, and have practiced running your energy, you may now begin your psychic explorations. Here are some tools and techniques to help you on your clairvoyant journey.

Always begin by running your energy and cleaning and resetting your chakras as described in Exercise 11. This practice clears your energy field of distractions and moves your attention up into your spiritual centers where you can read clairvoyantly.

CREATING A VIEWING SCREEN AND
VISUALIZING IMAGES

We use a **"viewing screen"** to visualize images and information, so that is the first thing you can do. From the center of your head, visualize a cinema screen, or any variety of screen you feel most comfortable using, and position it out in front of your sixth chakra maybe 18-24 inches or so. I use a regular movie screen image and put roses around it to help neutralize the information. But you can get creative and imagine any screen that works for you. Some people just use roses instead and ask to see the information on the surface of the rose. That is also fine. Just play with a few images and see what you like best. It is, however, always important to use a screen or rose because they create separation between you and what you are exploring clairvoyantly. This tool will prevent you from merging with the pictures and associated emotional charge of the content you are "reading."

Learning to read clairvoyantly is a lot like learning to ride a bike. At first it feels strange perching up high on a bike seat and balancing on two skinny tires and then pedaling fast enough not to fall over. Then try to turn a corner too? How is that even possible? I remember many skinned knees when I was learning to ride my first two-wheel bike. The same can be said when you sit down, run your energy and rise up to the center of your head in preparation for a reading. If you try really hard to "see something" psychically, you will go into effort and re-activate the 3rd chakra, tumbling back down into it. This is called **"losing your space"** in the psychic schools. It's like falling off your bike but without the skinned knees. So, in the beginning when you first start reading, it's helpful to take the pressure off and adopt an attitude of playfulness. Let go and notice the energy rather than staring at your screen with knitted brows. That will help you to remain seated in your psychic center in this higher frequency domain with full access to the spiritual information residing there.

I am going to give you some training wheels to help take the pressure off and give you experience viewing images on your screen. The purpose is to avoid freezing when you wait to *see something clairvoyantly*. The following exercise will help you become accustomed to using your mind's eye so that after a little practice—when you ask yourself a question—your inner self can deliver the images to your viewing screen without triggering common beginner's performance anxiety. This is supposed to be fun so let's get rolling and have some psychic fun!

PRACTICE VIEWING IMAGES ON YOUR SCREEN

Run your energy, as usual, and reset your chakras for a reading (1st chakra 10%, 2nd chakra 10%, 3rd chakra 60%, 4th chakra 60%, 5th chakra 80%, 6th chakra 80%, 7th chakra 80%). Stabilize your attention in the center of your head. (Remember to pull back from your forehead so your attention is stabilized in the psychic center as far back as the tops of your ears.) Create your viewing screen in your mind's eye and put some roses beside it to neutralize the energy. Begin to "ask yourself" to see various objects on your screen. When you are finished viewing one image, drain the image off the bottom of the screen into a rose, and then move the rose outside of your aura and destroy it, thereby releasing the energy and recycling it. Then move on to visualizing the next image. Here are some examples, but feel free to be creative and ask yourself whatever object you want to appear on your screen:

- "If I could see a lavender rose on my screen, what would it look like?" Allow the rose to appear on your screen and notice what it looks like. Don't judge anything, even if you can't see the rose clearly. Just acknowledge to yourself the aspects of the lavender rose *you are seeing* and move on. Drain it from the bottom of your screen into a rose and destroy the rose. Go to the next image.
- "If I could see a small red rose bud on my screen, what would it look like?" Again, notice the image and acknowledge your success visualizing the red rose bud on your screen. Drain it into a rose and destroy the image.
- "If I could see a stick figure man smoking a pipe, what would it look like?"
- "If I could see a sailboat floating on the water, what would it look like?"
- "If I could see a black dog with a red ball in its mouth, what would it look like?"
- Invent your own objects and continue viewing them by asking yourself to see them on your screen.

Keep going for about 5-10 minutes and practice this for several days. While it may seem tedious, it will help you build confidence in viewing images on your screen without the extra pressure of seeking clairvoyant information from your inner self. You are building your picture-making muscles so that viewing images on your screen becomes second nature. When you are finished with each session, fill with a gold sun, bend forward and balance your energy by touching the ground. Soon you will master seeing with your inner eyes and, like learning to ride a bike, you will always have this handy visualization skill at the ready for your future clairvoyant explorations.

EXPLORING AN ISSUE CLAIRVOYANTLY

Now that you have become familiar using your viewing screen and have practiced seeing images appear on it using your mind's eye, it's time to take the training wheels off and put the rubber on the road. To exercise your clairvoyance, ask yourself a clear question and wait for your inner self to answer by sending you messages on your screen in the form of images, symbols, energy or words. As always, run your energy as described in Exercise 11 and set your chakras for a clairvoyant reading. Seat yourself in the psychic center of your sixth chakra and create your viewing screen out in front of you. Select a simple question you would like to explore. From the center of your head, **"ask yourself"** the question and notice what appears on your screen.

Let's consider a hypothetical example. Say you meet a woman in your new painting class—we will call her "Jackie"—and for some unknown reason, you feel annoyed by her. You thought about it and can't come up with a reason why she is so irritating to you. You want to enjoy your painting class and not be distracted by this annoyance, so you decide to explore this issue clairvoyantly. Run your energy, set up your viewing screen and begin asking yourself some questions:

- Ask to see the image of a rose on your screen.
- Ask the rose to light up the color of the emotion "Jackie" evokes.
- It lights up a bright red. Ask what emotion that color represents.
- You get it is anger and frustration.
- See the red rose dissolve and drain off the bottom of your screen into another rose. Move that rose away (out of your aura) and destroy it.
- Ask for a picture or symbol to appear on your screen which

represents the source of the unconscious conflict you have with Jackie which evokes anger and frustration in you.

- You see an image of a woman sitting behind a desk with an apple on it. You realize this image represents a female teacher.
- Ask yourself if you know or have known a female teacher that has irritated you or caused frustration. You realize your 3rd grade teacher, Mrs. Crabwort, was always a pain in the neck. You remember she had an annoying voice and rude manner which always bothered you.
- Again, see these images dissolve and drain off the bottom of your screen into a rose. Move the rose away and destroy it.
- Ask yourself, what about Jackie brings up old feelings about your 3rd grade teacher?
- On your screen, you see an image of a head projecting sharp sound waves from its mouth. You realize Jackie's voice sounds just like your old teacher, Mrs. Crabwort's voice. When Jackie talks, it stimulates the same old irritation you felt toward your 3rd grade teacher when you were a kid.
- Thoroughly clean your screen with a rose and then destroy the rose.
- Ask for an image of yourself on your screen. Ask where you hold this anger and annoyance in your body. You see your stomach area light up on your screen. Use a vacuum rose to clean out this energy in your stomach as represented on your screen. Move your vacuum rose out of your aura and destroy it. On your screen, fill your stomach area with a color that is pleasant and relaxing for you.
- Suggest to yourself that Jackie will no longer evoke frustration in you because she is a different person than Mrs. Crabwort. That you will enjoy painting class with Jackie without any further discomfort or distraction.
- When you are finished, drop your entire screen in a rose and destroy it outside your aura.
- Call in a golden sun at your crown and let the neutral energy fill your body. Bend forward and balance by touching the ground.

Your questions can be about anything, so be creative. There is no rigid format or right way to read issues so relax and be spontaneous. It's smart to begin with easier questions that aren't emotionally charged. My example shows how you might use your psychic tools such as roses— on your screen to receive information clairvoyantly— as well as "vacuum roses" (or "sticky roses" if you prefer), which clear and neutralize the pictures and energy on your screen. I encourage you to develop your own clairvoyant style and be adventurous. It is important, however, to always finish with a healing and to refill your aura with earth energy and golden cosmic energy.

Another way to explore questions which involve yourself, is to **visualize a mirror image of yourself on your screen** and start with easy-ish questions. For example, you might say, "I've had a bit of a spacy day. I was slow leaving the traffic signal this morning and a driver blasted their horn at me. Where am I carrying the energy of this jarring experience?" Then watch and see what area of your body or energy field lights up out on your screen. If you don't see anything, use the **"purple dust"** tool. Ask the question again and sprinkle a little imaginary purple dust over the top of your head on your screen and see where it lands. "Oh! I see it's around my stomach area and my chest tensed. I'm carrying it in my stomach and chest." Then you might ask, "Is this bringing up other uncomfortable memories of similar experiences?" For yes and no answers, **I use a green light for yes, and a red light for no** So, I imagine a traffic light on my screen and ask the question and see which lights up. You can develop your own system of symbols that works best for you. Keep asking questions until you are satisfied with your exploration.

Then finish with a healing. You may use a **vacuum or sticky rose** to clean out the car horn noise and aggressive energy in the stomach and chest area. Gently vacuum out (or wipe away) any old pictures that got triggered by the experience and bubbled to the surface. Run the rose around those areas of the imaginary you on your screen and see all of the energy move into the rose. Next, move the rose out of your aura and burst it into gold dust. Remember to replenish your energy. Every time you release energy, draw in a golden sun of cosmic energy from over your head and pull in more earth energy through your feet. Watch it flow to the places you healed and refresh your entire energy field.

If it feels easier, you may do the self-healing from your screen instead. Visualize earth energy coming in "mini-you's" feet and cosmic gold energy coming in her crown. Then fill in the entire body and energy field with those neutral healing vibrations. As you give the "representative you" on your screen a healing, your own system will follow suit and heal you simultaneously. When you feel finished with your session, drop your screen in a big rose, move it out of your energy field and burst it into gold dust. Then bend forward and balance your energy by touching the ground. You can ask just about anything but it's good to start with simple questions with easier, more manageable topics.

Other psychic devices we use to help us get information are **gauges and timelines**. On your screen, you can create a simple gauge with an arrow which points from zero to 100 percent. Then ask your quantitative questions such as, what percentage of my energy is tied up in solving other people's problems? Or how much progress have I made toward healing my fear of garden gnomes? Whatever quantitative questions you have work well with these kinds of visual tools. Look at your gauge and see what it indicates.

0 Percent   100 Percent

Regarding timelines, you can ask questions regarding the duration of situations or when a particular condition was set in motion, by referring to a mental image of a timeline. For example, "How long have I carried my father's depression? Oh, I see from my timeline that I started this six years ago. That makes sense because that's when mom died." You get the picture.

Another helpful tool is what we call "**amusement**" which is the energy of lightness and levity. I can't tell you how many times a readee comes to me and expects a profound interpretation of their condition and instead I suggest comedy—funny friends, books, movies and enjoyable activities. Enjoying the easy energy of amusement and levity helps to shift the energy from a stuck place of seriousness and get it moving again.

When you first start "reading" in the format just described, you may not see anything and feel discouraged that you're not clairvoyant—that this system won't work for you because visualization is too challenging. Don't be discouraged; this is very common. Go back to the "Creating and Destroying Roses" exercise and do that every day for a few weeks before you try again to read clairvoyantly. The ability to visualize images in your mind's eye can be developed through repeated exercise. In clairvoyance, you are simply requesting information be delivered from your soul to your conscious mind. And you definitely have a soul; it is a primary part of you, so you definitely can develop your natural clairvoyance. This work re-activates the communication system between your soul and your personality, but that system might have gotten dusty from lack of use. It takes time to dust it off and re-activate the wiring. So, be patient with yourself.

BLOWING PICTURES

You can also attract pictures out of your energetic space and examine them on the surface of an imaginary rose which takes the place of your viewing screen. (Using your screen is fine. Using a rose is just another way you can read and heal pictures because it reduces emotional charge, making your explorations more pleasant.) I will offer a few more reading tools which you may employ in your readings to support your clairvoyance.

First, make sure you have run and cleared your energy, reset your chakras for a reading, and have your crown set at gold. Stay in the center of your head and select a memory which is uncomfortable but not overwhelming. Start with easier issues first so the practice of "blowing pictures" is not an unpleasant activity that you avoid. When you have decided on an experience from your past, ask to see a representative picture of it on the surface of your rose. You may see a symbol, or energy or a more literal picture representing the experience. Don't judge what you see, just go with it. You can ask all energy held in your body or energy system associated with this experience be attracted out of your space and absorbed into the rose. You may ask yourself what you need to know about this picture—what unconscious belief has been blocking you from processing this experience and moving on? See what lights up on your rose. What nugget of truth have you learned from your clair-voyant exploration of this picture? How has your perspective changed as a result? When you are satisfied the rose has absorbed the picture, the associated emotion, and that you have explored the information to your satisfaction, then move the rose out of your aura and burst it into gold dust, thereby blowing the picture. Your truth will return to you over your crown chakra and be reabsorbed into your energy system and stored ap-propriately. You may craft an affirmation or intention that supports your movement forward. Always refill with healing energy.

These sessions are important to journal because you can track the changes in your life as a result of blowing pictures. An old mold of frozen energy was just released and that part of you that was occupied by the event is freed back into present time. How has your perspective changed? Did you adopt an affirmation to help support the shift and move into a new, more positive perspective? Watch for circumstances to change in your life as a result of this healing. It's fun to track and very transforma-tive.

WHAT TO DO WHEN YOU GET REALLY STUCK

Occasionally, when I'm trying to examine something clairvoyantly, I draw a complete blank. You can check your chakra settings and come back up to the center of your head if this happens. You may have "lost your space" and fallen back down to the third chakra. Simply take the ex-press elevator back up to the center of your head, set your crown chakra at gold, and run the gold energy for a minute or two. This will help you return to neutrality so it's easier to read. You might re-state your question in a different way. A trick we sometimes use is to say, "I'm not seeing anything yet, but if I could see the answer to this question, what would it look like?" That can take the pressure off and stimulate the answers to come forward. You may be looking at an issue that really jangles you and your system goes into resistance. It's fine to set it aside for a while and pick it back up when you're ready. You might journal about the issue a bit to break yourself in and choose another day and time when you feel ready. Be gentle with yourself. It will take some time to become confident in seeing clairvoyantly so be patient. That's why clairvoyant training programs are, at a minimum, one year long.

When we are learning to read, sometimes we try so hard that it blocks the flow of psychic messages and we become self-conscious and intimidated, making it hard to perform. It's fine to take the pressure off and just use the system for fun and without high expectations to begin with. By not pressuring ourselves and choosing instead to relax and have fun, the images can come forward and be noticed by that aspect of your consciousness that is easygoing and spontaneously intuitive.

On the other hand, sometimes we *do see an image* and then second guess ourselves about it. Work to trust what you see, even if it seems strange or even ridiculous. Once I was reading a friend and at the end of the session, she asked if there was anything else she should know before we closed the reading. On my screen, I saw an aerial image of the east corner of her backyard, then I saw a kangaroo, then I saw two thumbs-up. I *really* didn't want to report that. But my policy is "say what you see" so I reported the nonsensical images. She said that made perfect sense because she was considering whether or not to invest in a trampoline and put it in that corner of her backyard for exercise. That was both funny and validating. Later she purchased a great big trampoline which she still enjoys to this day. Trust your clairvoyance.

FOREIGN ENERGY IN THE AURA

In the course of our lifetimes, we are in contact with many people and in various kinds of relationships. In families, romantic relationships, professional relationships or friendships, we often pick up each other's energy and carry it without realizing it. There's nothing wrong with other people's energy but it isn't ours—it's foreign to our system no matter how close we are to that person. Our system functions best running its own energy. Carrying other people's energy means we carry many of their opinions, tendencies, and emotions too, especially if we tend to be empathic and feel others' emotions in our own bodies (also known as clairsentience). Naturally, this can cause confusion and difficulty knowing what our views and choices are independent of those around us. Clearing other people's energy from our fields helps us to **"own our space"** and reduce confusion.

To remove another person's energy from your field and send it back to them doesn't mean you don't care about them or don't want to be in a relationship with them. On the contrary, it helps to create some space between you both so it's easier to interact from your own individual position and perspective. The following exercise uses **vacuum roses** to help you release other people's energy. First let's talk about other forms of foreign energy we often carry in our auras that we can also remove with the rose exercise.

Growing up in families, in communities, and in nations of people, we are raised within familial, cultural, educational and religious systems which teach certain beliefs that we incorporate into our energy systems in the form of pictures. In addition, the constant barrage of media messaging about physical appearance, financial success, and what we should buy materially provides constant programming about what we should value and strive for. Families also have implicit and explicit messaging about what's valued in that family and what the child must do to win favor and validation. Attaining the highest grades in the class, consistently winning at sports, and achieving honors in a multitude of competitions are the measuring sticks parents and schools often use to encourage kids to do their best. If excessive, these external standards can leave many kids feeling that who they are naturally is of no consequence and their own particular interests and aptitudes may be overlooked altogether. Progressing through the educational system can train us out of our own individuality and program us to move through the world in a cookie-cutter sort of way. All of these systems, to some extent, condition us to believe certain things and act in certain ways which may not reflect our own authentic self. We call this **programming**. These constant messages from our environment form pictures in our energy field which can cause confusion and a feeling of being out of touch with our true selves. Programming can also be removed, bit by bit, with the following rose exercise.

Exercise 12
Removing Foreign Energy From Your Aura

*Close your eyes and breathe restfully for a minute or two. Run your energy and reset your chakras for a reading. Affirm your grounding to the planet and your free flow of cosmic energy entering your crown.

*Create a rose in front you and outside your aura. Give it the superpower of attracting foreign energy out of your energy field like a magnet.

*Name the person or type of programming you will be removing from your energy field.

*Give that rose a grounding cord which reaches to the center of the planet.

*Now ask that rose to match the frequency of the person or programming you are removing from your space. Trust the rose follows your intention easily and effortlessly. Notice what color your rose becomes. This is the vibration of the foreign energy you will be releasing from your aura. Because like attracts like, it will give the rose the magnetic charge needed to attract this energy out of your aura.

*Ask the rose to gently vacuum out that energy and absorb it—together with the associated opinions, tendencies, and emotions you have been carrying. Watch it flow out of your field and into the rose. See if you can notice where it is held in your body and/or energy field. Notice if you feel a shift of energy in that location as the rose attracts it out of your space. You may see pictures that belong to that person or particular programming leave your space and enter the rose. Trust it is happening whether you see it for now or not.

*Now ask that any pictures you hold in your aura which unconsciously gave that energy permission to sit in your field, also be identified and released into the rose.

*When you feel complete, see the foreign energy drain from the rose blossom down the stem to the center of the planet. The earth will recycle the energy.

*When you are ready, destroy the rose and any energy of your own will be returned to your crown chakra where it is sorted and stored properly in your system.

*Call in a golden sun from over your head and let the high gold replenish your energy field and in particular, heal the area in which you were holding the foreign energy. Draw in some earth energy through your feet and allow it to re-ground you. Take a few deep breaths and bend forward and balance your energy by touching the ground.

It may now occur to you that you probably have some of your own energy held in other people's auras as well. You can do this same exercise but put your own energy in the vacuum rose. Picture a particular person out on your screen and attract your energy out of their aura using your rose. They do not need to be present for this exercise to be effective. Follow the same procedure. Calling back your energy frees the other person to be themselves and enhances your energy by owning it for yourself.

THE CROWN CHAKRA—KNOW THYSELF

The crown chakra's purpose and function is to know what is true. It is the portal through which our conscious minds receive information and guidance from our inner self and the non-physical dimensions. In meditation, moving up to the crown chakra and exploring the expansive energy of your spiritual self and your soul's wisdom is one of the finer gifts of being human. Breathwork, meditation and prayer work is amplified when done from the 7th chakra at your crown.

In a reading space, we are seeing images using the clairvoyance of the 6th chakra but often pop up to the 7th chakra for interpretations of that particular image or symbol seen psychically. We do this without thinking about it, but it is the natural pattern of discerning the information in a person's aura to "know" what it means. Reading is a dance of back and forth between these two chakras that produce a reading not only rich in visual information but also context and meaning. Exercising the 7th chakra and having open communication between your conscious personality and soul self will provide day-to-day guidance for balanced living and spiritual fulfillment.

The following exercise will help you move up to the 7th chakra and engage in conversations with your own soul. The more you practice this the easier it is to shift to these high frequencies of the crown chakra and stabilize your focus there. When you surrender to the ease and flow of your expansive spiritual nature, you open the doors of inner perception and your own unique knowing of truth.

I think 99 times and find nothing. I stop thinking, swim in silence, and the
truth comes to me.
–Albert Einstein

Exercise 13
Rise up to Your Crown—Talking with Your Soul

*Close your eyes and take a few deep, cleansing breaths. Allow your body to relax and your awareness to turn inward. Be in the center of your head once again. From here, acknowledge your grounding cord and the support you are receiving from the earth.

*Now see your crown chakra at the top of your head drawing in cosmic energy vibrating at a soft golden color. Just explore this high frequency gold energy and enjoy its soothing properties.

*Visualize the gold energy flowing gently through your crown chakra and lightly filling your body, chakras, and aura. Running this free flow of gold energy through your system helps to maintain neutrality during the day and connect with the high vibrations of your soul.

*Now rise up to just above your crown and rest your attention above your body. Invite your soul, your inner most spiritual identity, to share its spiritual essence and energy with you. Allow a soft focus here. Just float gently above your body and let go. Feel the vibration, the tone of your soul self.

*You may repeat an affirmation or prayer or simply enjoy the beautiful energy of your inner spiritual realm. You may ask your soul what messages or guidance it has for you that day. See what comes. Maybe you get impressions, feelings, images, ideas, symbols or just a sense of calming reassurance. Sometimes the guidance comes through later in the day in the form of synchronicities or messages either direct or subtle. Be open to however your soul guidance emerges and thank it.

*When you feel complete, gently bring your attention back to the room and open your eyes. Bend forward and touch the ground, balancing and resetting your energy.

"Know Thyself" is inscribed above the gates at Delphi in Greece. Your crown chakra is your own personal gateway to knowing what is true and who you are. Additionally, our soul is the original and highest aspect of ourselves—the part that is forever immersed in God consciousness, without distraction. Our entire self, including the more mundane aspects of our personality, are also unceasingly immersed in the light of God, but these parts are very distracted by our busy lives and egoic attachments. When we engage in prayer, our soul is the first place we register that elevated awareness and can most easily receive guidance without egoic distortion. So, by learning to raise our vibration up into the higher causal realms, and to fortify our relationship and communication with our own souls, we simultaneously strengthen our communication with God.

I will now introduce the concept of "seniority" which means to stand back up and claim your spiritual sovereignty after blowing pictures, false beliefs or removing another person's energy and influence from your system. Prior to clearing these energetic influences, these pictures, at least partly, drove your emotional life and decisions and may have been quite dominant forces in your life. But they weren't true representations of who you are as a spirit and in truth, what you want to create. By removing these influences and reconnecting with what is true for you in present time, you achieve **spiritual seniority**. Every time you blow a picture or remove energetic obstacles along your inner path, acknowledge your seniority and appreciate your sovereignty consciously. Piece by piece, you call yourself back into present time and occupy your full field of consciousness as the unique spirit you are. Celebrate this and journal about your successes and growth.

One way to keep your crown chakra tuned-up is to imagine a **golden marble** on top of your head rolling around the circumference of the crown chakra (or its entry point to your head). This clears foreign energy and influences so you can **"own your crown"** and spiritual identity.

You can also stabilize your spiritual presence in a room or building by **"owning and grounding the room."** Simply see golden cords of energy shooting up from your crown chakra and connecting to each corner of the ceiling. (I like to visualize them like Spider Man's filament cords shooting out quickly and effortlessly but from my crown instead of my hands.) The second half of this technique is to send golden cords from your crown to all the corners of the floor and then send those cords down to the center of the planet and ground them. Owning and grounding the room is a powerful statement of your right to create and express yourself in a space using your own personal vibration. It does not prevent others from owning the room at their own unique vibration or mean you are going into competition with others regarding the space. Everyone can own and ground the room for themselves without interfering with other people's sovereignty in the building. It simply is your statement of ownership of your own experience at your own unique vibration in that place and at that time. I recommend doing this daily at home, at work or other significant spaces and notice how you feel differently. For me, I feel confident, grounded, and have permission to express myself authentically in a safe space. Try it and see what you find.

I have covered several concepts and energy exercises which will take some time to acquaint yourself with and begin using. Allow the time and don't try to rush things. Listen to yourself and track how you feel as you travel this path. Once you have mastered the exercises, you can modify them a bit to fit your own style. My mode of running my energy and reading is a little different than how I was trained because it is my own unique expression of clairvoyance and spiritual healing. Continue to journal and to pay attention to the dreams you have at night. They will provide valuable insights to your own particular mode of operating spiritually and what works best for you.

THE READING LINE AND CLAIRVOYANT SCHOOLS

In 2001, I spent one year at Aesclepion's Clairvoyant Training Program (CT)–after having completed their three, seven-week long pre-requisite meditation classes. I graduated from Aesclepion and enjoyed the benefits of working clairvoyantly with my own energy for personal development. My Reiki healing practice also improved with my new and more sophisticated understanding of the human energy system. Later I realized I wanted to do intuitive readings professionally, so I invested another three years of training at Psychic Horizons in San Francisco (aka the Church of Natural Grace). This entailed three, seven-week pre-requisite meditation classes, 18 months of beginning and advanced clairvoyant training, and an optional six-month apprenticeship program which I extended to one year. All tallied, I completed four years of training.

A formal program is a wonderful way to get professional training in the most comprehensive way. All of the energy awareness exercises and reading instruction will methodically build your skills and confidence. If you enjoy this work and have practiced these energy exercises on your own but want additional guidance and support from an experienced clairvoyant instructor, I strongly recommend enrolling in a professional clairvoyant training program. The Berkeley Psychic Institute (BPI) is the original clairvoyant training program and it spawned several other psychic schools that are based on the same model. My personal favorite is Psychic Horizons in San Francisco. I found the experience, commitment and compassion of all the Psychic Horizons instructors to be exceptional. If you decide you would like to help other people through clairvoyant readings, completion of a professional program is essential. Formal training and guidance will ensure you can conduct clairvoyant sessions competently and responsibly. (See the Other Resources section at the back of this book.) These programs also offer remote classes enabling people to participate from all over the world (and safely during the COVID 19 pandemic).

Learning to Read in a Clairvoyant School

What exactly happens in the clairvoyant training program setting? How do students learn to read? Each week you attend formal classes at each level of the program. There are also multiple weekly readings in which to participate.

In-person reading sessions are set up in the following way: the readee sits in a room with at least two or more students sitting opposite them in a "reading line." The most experienced reader will be the "center chair" and facilitate the reading. The readee can state their question and the center chair will ask them to repeat their full name out loud three times and watch the readee's crown chakra to see what vibration (color) it is set at. The center chair will match that same color at their crown and ask the reading line to match it as well. This tunes each reader into the readee's vibration like tuning in a radio. It's fun reading on a line and you can actually feel when the line is all matching the same vibration at their crown. When I matched the reading line vibration, I actually felt it in my body, like a Lego clicking into place. If someone "loses their space" and falls off the reading line color at their crown, the center chair can feel it and will ask the line to reset at the chosen vibration. This is very important because if everyone is matching the same vibration, they will begin seeing many of the same pictures and reading within the same dimension of information. This validates the new students by confirming to them that they are actually "seeing clairvoyantly" and not just entertaining a random thought.

Each reader is given a part of the reading to lead, such as the chakra check-in or the rose reading at the beginning of the session. Then the center chair will proceed to read through each layer of the aura (from 1 to 7) to find relevant pictures and information regarding the readee's question. When they have finished reading a particular layer of the aura, they will ask the other students on the line if they have anything they would also like to share.

At the end, the center chair will ask if the readee would like a healing and if so, they will help to release pictures or stuck energy and help refill the person's energy field with cosmic and earth energy as well as one of the three universal healing energies. Through this entire experience, there is a "**control**" present in the room, a teacher or advanced student, assigned to help keep the room grounded, creating a safe space for the reading crew and readee.

Periodically during the reading, a teacher will come in and check to make sure everything is moving along alright. When the session is over and the readee has left, the teacher will come back in and ask each student what their **matching pictures** are. In every reading you will match at least one picture with the readee—a picture with similar content and emotional charge—which stimulates your own picture, potentially activating the related emotions. It's important to identify your matching pictures, explore them on your reading screen, and then de-energize them using a rose. This will prevent you from merging with or "falling into the picture" and losing your space. You may locate the "lit up" pictures in your aura by viewing them clairvoyantly, move them out of your aura (thereby separating from them), explore the information you are meant to understand about them, and then transform the energy, or "blow the picture." By studying the content of the picture from a neutral perspective and learning what it has to tell you about yourself, you will also learn fascinating information about where you've been on earth in other incarnations, how you got stuck, and what your truth is in present time. Clairvoyant programs provide a powerful opportunity to master the art of reading others, increase your own spiritual awareness, and transform your own energy for greater freedom in present time.

I have read thousands of people during my 18 year career and it's worth mentioning how their energy systems appear clairvoyantly. The multitude of pictures and thoughtforms residing throughout a person's aura appear like a patchwork of clothes, blocking out the light of their soul. Picture by picture, we can clear our auras of these heavy energetic "clothes" and cast them out, reflecting our sovereignty over the false beliefs we have harbored in our space, sometimes for multiple lifetimes. As we clear more and more of these energetic blocks, our light shines through, revealing our own unique beauty as a soul and illuminating our truth and path. To me, committing to an ongoing practice of healing and releasing energetic pictures and thoughtforms is of vital importance. With my "sight" clear and true, my soul can shine its light unobstructed and so contribute its own unique expression in the world without distortion. In addition, the pictures held in our energy fields invariably manifest more of the same unwanted, negative conditions due to the law of attraction~like attracts like. So if we desire a more positive and fulfilling life, clearing old pictures and thoughtforms from our auras is well worth the time and effort. We then manifest from a fresh energetic canvas.

Chapter 9

Personal & Collective Manifesting

You have been given perhaps the most awesome gift of all: the ability to project your thoughts outward into physical form.
—Seth (Roberts, Seth Speaks 6)

There is no shortage of books written on the law of attraction and manifesting your heart's desire so I will spare you the repetition. It is a relevant topic to address, however, because spiritual manifestation work is a system for focusing and projecting your creative psychic power into three-dimensional reality. I will explore both personal and collective manifesting and will also include a few techniques to support your work. But first, I have a few personal thoughts about manifestation work.

I have done my fair share of manifesting projects over the years. As I grow older (and hopefully wiser) I realize one of my shortfalls has been not to appreciate my life as it unfolds naturally. I am a gogetter when it comes to creating new and better conditions, so I am always reaching to improve my experience. As a very driven "third chakra culture," we're constantly reaching for the next and better thing. We have goals and are driven to achieve them one after the next, including spiritual manifestation goals and practices.

About five years ago, I experienced a recurring dream in which my spirit guides were trying to teach me something of significant importance. The dreams were early in the morning and always right before I woke up. I found myself maneuvering through a very challenging obstacle course. At the end of the course, I would pass the finish line and proclaim, "I did it!" Then, once again, my guides would shake their heads wearily, "no." I knew tomorrow I would have to try again. But what was I missing? Finally, one morning while navigating my dream obstacle course, my focus suddenly shifted. The experience was similar to studying those pictures containing dual images. You look at it one way and see the profile of a woman's face. But if you shift your focus, you suddenly see the image of an hourglass instead. This time rather than focusing on the obstacles and finish line, *I was keenly aware of the space in-between them. Suddenly the obstacle course was unimportant. In that moment, I was struck by a profound revelation. My challenge wasn't to surmount obstacles to achieve a goal, it was about presence.* It was about being present and showing up for life moment by moment no matter what situations or challenges lay before me. It was about valuing the space in-between; to grasp and appreciate the precious nature of each experience and to infuse it with my presence and awareness.

I share this because here in the Western world, we often try to control every element of our lives. Appreciating life on its own terms has become a lost art. Like my dream of the obstacle course, we may view every situation as something we must conquer. Or we might try to control or change the situation without deeper reflection about what that experience may be showing us. Many of us might use the law of attraction to re-engineer every aspect of our lives we find distasteful. Of course, to become aware of and release our unconscious beliefs that generate unnecessary hardship is important manifestation work, but constantly re-engineering our lives to create a perfect picture of life (according to our egos) may be excessive.

This brings me to my second thought. I have practiced the law of attraction and spiritual manifestation for years and know it works— but not always with certain projects. I searched my energy field for pictures and reasoned how my life would be so much better with the realization of this intended result, but it just wouldn't manifest. Ever. Well, now my hunch is that sometimes it shouldn't manifest— it's not in my best interest overall when looking at the bigger picture of my life.

I believe we are guided by our soul and the overarching purpose we have chosen for our life long before we incarnate. We have established soul agreements with ourselves at a deep level before each and every incarnation; agreements that provide the best pathway forward to learn the lessons we care about most. Seth says, "Each person chooses for himself the individual patterns <u>within which</u> he will create this personal reality. But inside these bounds are infinite varieties of actions and unlimited resources" (Roberts, *Nature of Personal Reality* 30). While we have a spectacular range of freedom to explore and create those things in our lives we care to experience, we may at times come up short in our efforts to manifest something in particular. But this may be in service to our highest good. Sometimes our ego—that part of our being which may not listen to the urgings of our spiritual self—may swoon over a particular thing we would like to manifest but it runs counter to our deeper purpose and the life lessons we have promised ourselves. With our best interest in mind, the guardrails are erected to keep our life on track. The object or condition desired fails to become manifest. This may feel frustrating or seem unfair but take heart. We are infinitely creative beings and though our project may not manifest in this particular line of reality, it may manifest in another probable reality—one which *is aligned with that condition you are working to create.*

Seth shares a wealth of information about probable realities and how infinite multiple lines of realities are continually operating simultaneously. In *The Unknown Reality, Volume Two,* I quote from session number 709:

> The world as you know it is the result of a complicated set of 'codes'…each locked in one to the other, each one in those terms dependent upon the others. Your precise perceived universe in all of its parts, then, results from coded patterns, each one fitting perfectly into the next. Alter one of these and to some extent you step out of that <u>context</u> (underlined). Any event of any kind that does not directly, immaculately intersect with your space-time continuum, does not happen, in your terms, but falls away. It becomes probable in your system but seeks its own 'level,' and becomes actualized as it falls into place in another reality whose 'coded sequence' fits its own. Period (Roberts, *Unknown Reality,* Volume 2).

Sometimes I wonder if these "codes" are reflected in our natal astrology charts. I believe that with the help of our spirit guides, we choose the time and place and family for each incarnation. Perhaps our astrological birth chart reflects the particular "curriculum" we have decided upon. It maps out our basic personality structure and propensities as well as the patterns of life we need to experience. We may create more varied experiences and conditions beyond the coding our chart represents, but the primary program perhaps overrides other inputs that would derail our main spiritual objectives. Energetically speaking, they are not resonant with and do not "directly and immaculately intersect" with our purpose within this specific line of reality.

Collectively, we may also have similar objectives en masse, together choosing in common a particular timeframe in which to incarnate. Certain collective challenges may be set up to offer us a group or mass experience where we must work together to find ways of responding and overcoming the challenge together. Seth states in session 708, that, "There are cycles in which consciousness forms earthly experience, and maps out historical sequences... Each system, of course, brings forth its own culture, 'technology,' art, and science" (Roberts, *Unknown Reality*, Volume 2).

We have the opportunity to play a part in the mass experience of our time and to make positive contributions that support our common goals and collective evolution. To be mindful of our interconnectedness and aware of the way our actions and manifestation work ripple out into the greater universe is of key importance. After all, our contemporaries—everyone and every creature—are truly our brothers and sisters in time. Together we make choices, moment by moment, which weave together our common history.

PERSONAL MANIFESTING

How might we best use the law of attraction to grow spiritually and unwind our stuck spots that create dysfunctional patterns in life? Are we and our reality that malleable? Seth says "you are given the most awesome gift of all: the ability to project your thoughts outward into physical form" (Roberts, *Seth Speaks* 6). If this is true, the first thing we need to be conscious of are our thought patterns and making sure they reflect what is true for us in present time and what we hope to create. Pictures held in our aura—emotionally charged records of our unresolved and sometimes traumatic experiences of the past—will play a role in forming our beliefs, whether conscious or unconscious, and give rise to self-sabotaging thinking with disappointing results. This is how our reality is *created unconsciously* but we do have the power to change our beliefs and related thoughts, thereby freeing ourselves into more fulfilling conditions.

Seth devotes much of his material to helping readers understand how they create their reality unconsciously. He also provides pointers about how to become aware of your thoughts, the beliefs from which they spring, and how to choose a different belief and new, healthier thoughts. There is a lag time, however, during which the original undesirable condition may continue to play out. This seems to prove that your reality is not only hopelessly unfortunate, but beyond your control and so unchangeable. But if you keep working with your beliefs over time, the new conditions will take root and eventually reveal your new, desirable condition. I quote Seth in *The Nature of Personal Reality*:

> Remember, even false beliefs will seem to be justified in terms of physical data, since your experience in the outside world is the materialization of those beliefs. So you must work with the raw materials of your ideas, even while your sense data may tell you that a given belief is obviously a truth. To change your experience or any portion of it, then, you must change your ideas. Since you have been forming your own reality all along, the results will follow naturally (Roberts, *Nature of Personal Reality* 29).

Seth offers his own method of shifting out of one's faulty beliefs and their related thought patterns/emotions, and into a new more beneficial circumstance by employing the power of one's imagination:

> There are various ways of altering the belief by substituting the opposite. One particular method is three-pronged. You generate the emotion <u>opposite</u> the one that arises from the belief you want to change, and you turn your imagination in the opposite direction from the one dictated by the belief. At the same time you consciously assure yourself that the unsatisfactory belief <u>is</u> an <u>idea</u> about reality and not an aspect of reality itself (Roberts, *Nature of Personal Reality* 63).

In this method, say for example you are lonely and would like more friends. Maybe you think that you are unlikeable and that's why you don't have more friends. You can shift these beliefs and your circumstance by employing Seth's three-pronged system. The first prong: Imagine what it would feel like to spend time with a new friend. Visualize laughing together and sharing your experiences and really feel the warmth and happiness of this new connection in your body. Again, this is the first prong which addresses the feeling aspect of a belief. Next, the second prong: Think about going places with this friend, having coffee, going to the movies or hiking, let your imagination roam and enjoy the things you want to do in your friendship. Notice how your new friend enjoys her time with you and finds you interesting and fun. You might imagine yourself going to her house for a party and meeting even more wonderful people. Daydream about the fun you are having with them and how they are enjoying your company. Again, this second prong engages your imagination to create a new mental picture of what you desire. Finally, the third prong: say to yourself, "See! I have made new friends. I am liked by my new friends and I'm no longer lonely." Affirm that your original belief—that you are an unlikeable person and don't have friends—"is *an idea about reality and not an aspect of reality itself.*" It can be washed away and replaced by the delightful feelings and thoughts you have been imagining, thereby creating a new inner experience which may now translate outwardly in the world of form.

Another point Seth often makes about manifesting a desired outcome is to activate and involve your nervous system by taking some physical action which supports it; engage consciously in a concrete action to move your dream into the world of form. For example, if our hypothetical lonely person is contacted out of the blue by an old acquaintance, she ought to take concrete action and return the call. She may also choose to move forward and join that hiking club she has been procrastinating about joining. Be proactive and engage in actions that affirm your manifestation work—"walk your talk" as they say. Finally, the use of affirmations in conjunction with these techniques is a powerful way to remain grounded in your intention and work daily on your manifesting endeavors.

Another powerful way to change unconscious, unproductive beliefs and thought forms is by creating a regular practice of actively blowing the pictures in your aura and adopting more positive and empowering beliefs to replace them. If you notice a negative pattern reactivated again in your life, identify the emotional tone of this problem. Then identify the thoughts you have been entertaining that are connected to this emotion. Then run your energy and enter into a clairvoyant space. Find the associated pictures in your aura. De-energize them and let them go. Chronic negative patterns always have corresponding unresolved pictures sitting in your aura. By using your clairvoyant space and tools offered in this book, you can systematically clean out your energy field of unwanted pictures and self-defeating clutter. In the back of the book, I have included some of my favorite affirmations. You may use them or create your own as you redirect your thinking from an old pattern into a new way of thinking that reflects where you want to head as a soul.

Cleaning house to remove negative patterns helps you to stop manifesting poor situations from unconscious beliefs. How do we know what to choose for our next *conscious manifesting effort*? Say you would like to actively create an exciting new element or circumstance in your life. Maybe you want to change careers or move to a new town. I suggest employing the help of your inner self and call a meeting with your soul at your seventh chakra. In meditation, you might ask your soul: "What shall I manifest next that serves my highest good and supports the good of the whole? What's my best next step?" You may be surprised to find answers quite different from what your ego has been cooking up. When we tap the impulses and desires of the ego alone, we will often seek to create objects and conditions concerning only the material realm. But to seek input from your higher self, you will begin manifesting events and fulfilling conditions which support the multidimensional aspects of your personhood as well—spiritual, mental, emotional, and physical.

Once you pose a question to your soul, the answer will be set in motion and be automatically attracted to you. Watch for synchronous events, impulses from your inner self, and flashes of insight. Once you *know* "your next step" (what you choose to work on in your conscious manifestation project) you can then set out to create it. Write it out clearly in the form of an intention.

Now that you have a clear manifestation goal, sit down and start working to discover and blow those pictures containing false beliefs and emotions that undermine your new creation. Explore on your screen, one by one, each picture by asking yourself, what do I carry in my energy field which runs counter to manifesting my next step as a spirit? Explore these pictures and beliefs clairvoyantly. Then move them out of your energy field and into a rose. Destroy the rose and release the pictures.

You may also notice that once you have written your intention, some fears and negative self-talk starts bubbling to the surface of your awareness. You may remember past experiences in which you tried something similar and had a bad experience. Use that information, don't suppress it! Sit down and blow your pictures related to that negative experience. Fill up again with the opposite feeling and craft a supporting affirmation. Blow your pictures day by day until they feel exhausted. Then, once again, write out your planned creation specifically and clearly. Your intention may have changed by the end of this process. It may be more robust and expansive.

When you are ready to begin your conscious manifestation work, I have provided a useful technique: the "mock-up" exercise we learn in clairvoyant training. It is a system for planting your seeds of manifestation so they may take root and grow. After you have performed your mock-up exercise, let it go and let the magic happen. Believe. Your third chakra, your ego, may stir up fear or uncertainty and urge you to fixate on this or perform your mockup multiple times. Resist the urge and instead validate your power as a creator.

Exercise 14
Creating a "Mock-up"

*Run your energy and clear and reset your chakras. (First chakra at 10%, Second chakra at 10%, Third chakra at 60%, Fourth chakra at 60%, Fifth chakra at 80%, Sixth chakra at 80% and Seventh chakra at 80%.) Set your crown chakra at gold.

*Visualize a light, floating, pink bubble outside your aura maybe four or five feet beyond your body. Imagine it is light as a helium balloon and create a string connecting it to the center of the planet so it won't float away.

*Now with your intention, state your mock-up—the condition or circumstance you are creating—and watch it float from you over to the bubble and become absorbed into it. You can mention any qualities or specifics and end by saying your intention is to "create this circumstance or its better." You may also intend that anything you care to put in this bubble but may have forgotten, will also be sent into this mock-up bubble so that nothing is missing or forgotten.

*Now create a golden cord and connect it to the bubble and your second chakra. Check to make sure your second chakra is in resonance with your mock-up. If you need to release any other impeding emotional energy, do so down your grounding cord.

*When you have checked for resonance, release the gold cord from the bubble and your second chakra. Lastly, cut the bubble's grounding cord and allow it to float away and begin its process of manifesting.

*Thank yourself for work well done and fill yourself up with a golden sun and bring in some earth energy through your feet. Bend forward and balance your energy by touching the ground.

COLLECTIVE MANIFESTING

I am reminded of Vine Deloria, Jr.'s wonderful explanation of the Native American perspective: that all people, all creatures, are connected and a part of a greater living universe. "We are in the truest sense possible, creators or co-creators with the higher powers, and what we do has immediate importance for the rest of the universe" (Deloria Jr. 46). Because everything is related and alive, finding one's place and proper action in any circumstance is important and is indeed that person's responsibility to the whole. This reminds me that it's not just "all about me" and what I want. We are all in this together and given the jam we are in on the planet now, it's of urgent importance that we shift our perspective from me to we and consider not only ourselves, but the collective good as well.

Collective manifestation is a form of **spiritual activism** we can all do to help heal violence and work to improve the many environmental and social problems we face together on planet earth. Lynne McTaggart's work with group intention and restoring peace is an excellent example of the impact we can have in the world when we work together. I consider this to be one of the most powerful forms of collective manifestation in which we can engage. By combining our individual creative power with others focused on the same intention, we boost our energy into an enormous, focused, positive force for change.

McTaggart's 2017 "American Peace Intention Experiment" results reflect the power of group intention to reduce violent crime by focusing on one of the highest crime neighborhoods in America. Between September 30 through October 5, 2017, McTaggart broadcast daily over Gaia television her "American Peace Intention Experiment" and invited viewers to join in and focus their intention during the same period.

The target identified for this experiment was the nation's highest crime neighborhood, the Natural Bridge Avenue in northern St. Louis, Missouri. Her study reports this neighborhood has a murder rate three times that of Chicago and fifteen times higher than NY City. The area suffering the worst concentration of violent crime in the Natural Bridge

Avenue area is Fairground, bordered by West Florissant Avenue in the north and East Natural Bridge Road in the south—this was established as the project's specific target.

The experiment's chosen focus was on violent crime alone, including rape, robbery, aggravated assault, and murder and to reduce this crime by, at minimum, 10 percent (McTaggart, Results of the American Peace Intention Experiment).

The University of California professor of statistics, Dr. Jessica Utts, studied four different sets of crime data in St. Louis for the period September 2014 through March 2018 including monthly property and violent crime (in St. Louis at large and separately, Natural Bridge Avenue in Northern St. Louis, and the targeted Fairground neighborhood). She compared the property and violent crime data and trends before the experiment with the six months following the experiment for these locations.

Utts found that *crime overall* had increased in the six-month period following the experiment due to an increase in *property crime. But violent crime in the Fairground neighborhood declined, and by much more than ten percent.* The results were stunning. I quote from McTaggart's website:

> Only Fairground's violent crime the target of our intention – had a lower incidence than forecast. Then, when Dr. Utts mapped the general historical trends of crime starting with September 2014, although violent crime in Fairground had been steadily increasing, that general trend reversed immediately after our Intention Experiment (McTaggart, Results of the American Peace Intention Experiment).

In fact, *violent crime, which was the target of the experiment, had decreased over the same period by 43 percent.* Utts also found that during the same October through March time period the year before, police statistics showed 44 violent crimes. This number dropped to 25 after the experiment. Additionally, the Fairground neighborhood was the only neighborhood along North Bridge Avenue that experienced a large decrease in violent crime. On McTaggart's website, the scientific methodology and findings are explained clearly. For more information, please refer to her website

(McTaggart, Results of the American Peace Intention Experiment).

The many global peace intention experiments conducted by McTaggart's over the years have consistently found impressive results for those areas targeted by the group. However, they also discovered a "mirror effect" whereby the participants involved in "focusing positive intentions" also experienced positive changes in their own lives. Participants reported better relationships with others following their involvement with one of McTaggart's experiments. I quote McTaggart from her book, *The Bond*:

In September 2008, I ran an experiment with 15,000 participants from sixty countries, examining whether 'group mind' has the power to lower violence and restore peace. The plan was to have readers all over the world join forces on our website to send peace to a particular war-torn area— in this instance, Sri Lanka.

In a survey I conducted of participants after completion of the experiment, some 46 percent said they noticed longterm changes in their relationships with others after the experiment. The group experience apparently helped them to feel more love in general, whether or not they knew the recipient. More than 25 percent felt more love for their loved ones or for people they normally dislike or argue with, 41 percent felt more love for with [sic] all those with whom they came into contact, and 19 percent found they were getting along better with perfect strangers (McTaggart, *The Bond* 178).

I think a common belief is that if we give something to another person, we then have less ourselves. These experiments suggest the opposite is true when it comes to group intention work. *We gain more personal benefit through our acts of spiritual generosity.* We might further surmise that the personal benefits grow each time we work selflessly for the collective good. What a welcome demonstration of how we can help others while also improving our own lives and relationships.

I encourage readers to explore group intention work and consider getting involved with others to help manifest a healthier and more evolved world. I recommend McTaggart's books: *The Field, The Bond, The*

Intention Experiment, and *The Power of Eight* to learn more.

There are also numerous global meditations organized by various spiritual groups with a specific issue as the focus. People are invited to join in for the same predetermined time period to boost the power of their group manifestation objective. Some target a particular issue or location for a specific purpose; others correspond with a significant astrological event happening at that time, lending a beneficial "astrological opportunity" to support a particular collective intention. It's worth checking out and fun to get involved. These activities *do* create change and it feels great to connect with others in such a positive way.

THE EARTH CONNECTION

Physically speaking, earth itself has its own kind of gestalt consciousness. If you <u>must</u>, then think of that earth consciousness as grading (spelled) upward in great <u>slopes</u> of awareness from relatively 'inert' particles of dust and stone through the mineral, vegetable, and animal kingdoms. Even then, remember that those kingdoms are not so separate after all. Each one is highly related to each of the others. Nothing happens in one such kingdom that does not affect the others. A great, gracious cooperation exists between those seemingly separate systems. If you will remember that even atoms and molecules have consciousness, then it will be easier for you to understand that there is indeed a certain kind of awareness that unites these kingdoms...

The environment itself is conscious. (Roberts, *Unknown Reality, Volume 2,* Session 705)

Remembering our place in the whole of life—acknowledging our true home within the living universe—will help us to reconnect consciously with ourselves and the earth. I repeat Deloria, Jr.'s words, "The living universe requires mutual respect among its members...The willingness of entities to allow others to fulfill themselves, and the refusal of any entity to intrude thoughtlessly on another, must be the operative principle of this universe" (Deloria Jr. 50-1). To fully appreciate the earth and all of her creatures means to humble ourselves and to acknowledge that all life matters. The earth, herself, matters. If we join together and use the power of our collective intention, we can heal ourselves and our planet. If together, we commit to live consciously and with humility, we can turn the tide and thrive as one community of life upon the earth.

I have included a wonderful meditation for a blessing of the earth. It is inspired by "Meditation on Twin Hearts," presented in the late Master Choa Kok Sui's book *Miracles Through Pranic Healing* (Sui 333-6). I find sending love and healing to the earth and all of her creatures to be both tender and powerful. It is also a wonderful meditation to do together with others on Earth Day or whenever the inspiration strikes.

This is a very sweet form of manifesting for the collective good—sending healing for the earth and all life on the planet.

Exercise 15
An Earth Blessing

*Run your energy lightly and ground yourself to the center of the planet. Call in cosmic gold energy through your crown chakra and seat your attention in the center of your head. Acknowledge your positive intention to send healing to the earth.

*Put your hand on your HEART and bless the earth with love and healing. You may visualize a small earth out in front of you. From your heart, send love to the earth and visualize this healing energy flowing over to the planet from your heart—watch the aura of the earth glow a brighter and brighter golden pink color.

*Now rise up to your CROWN and seat your awareness there. From your crown chakra, send the earth healing light and wisdom from your soul. Again, visualize the energy and messages of the blessing moving from your crown chakra to the earth out in front of you. Feel the meaning and love of these words as you do this.

*You may create a BLESSING of your own and speak it now, watching the loving energy of the words traveling to the small planet out in front of you. Here is a blessing I use which might inspire you:

From the light of my soul, I send love and
good will to the earth and all her creatures.
From my soul I ask all cruelty and selfishness be
dissolved into the light of loving kindness.
From my soul I send the loving intention
that every human is inspired to do
generous things for each other, for all
animals, and for the earth herself.

From my soul, I send wisdom and compassion to
all life on earth so that the desire to live peacefully and
with kindness rests in the heart of all beings.

*See the little earth out in front of you glowing brighter still with
an aura of gold and pink, pulsating with loving kindness.

*Now, from both your HEART and CROWN chakra, offer the
earth one final blessing:

"May the earth and all her
creatures rest in the protection of
infinite love."

*Gently bring your attention back to the room and take a few
deep breaths. Appreciate the love and healing you have gener-
ated from the light of your own being. Open your eyes. Bend
forward and balance your energy by touching the ground.

Of course, you can create your own healing meditation for the earth.
Use your imagination to create a loving blessing which you give to the
earth when you feel it is needed. This is a powerful way to shift energy
and raise your vibration while giving back to the earth in gratitude for all
that she gives you.

Chapter 10

Spontaneity and Seth's "Magical Approach"

*To 'let go' is to trust the spontaneity of your
own being, to trust your own energy and power
and strength, and to abandon yourself to the
energy of your own life.*
—Seth (Roberts, *Way Toward Health* 268)

Seth focuses a great deal on spontaneity and the important force it can be in our lives. It's the uninhibited flow of activity we experience as children while playing and it is the power of our own natural rhythm and flow as adults—an ease and effortlessness that can free us back to authentic selves and our creative nature. The quote from *The Way Toward Health* at the beginning of this chapter emphasizes the value of "letting go" and experiencing your own spontaneous nature. Not just for relaxation and enjoyment, but for improved health—physical, mental, emotional and spiritual as well.

...To abandon yourself, then, to the power of your own life, is to rely upon the great forces within and yet beyond nature that gave birth to the universe and to you.

One of the very first steps toward mental, physical, emotional and spiritual health is precisely that kind of abandonment, that kind of acceptance and affirmation.

The will to live is also inbred into each element of nature, and if you trust your own spontaneity, then that will to be is joyfully released and expressed through all of your activities. It can also quite literally wash depression and suicidal tendencies away. Those feelings do indeed encourage expression of consciousness, and release intuitive information that may otherwise be buried beneath tensions and fears (Roberts, *Way Toward Health* 268-9).

I incorporate the importance of spontaneity and what Seth terms "the magical approach" because it is another way of experiencing reality—including solving problems and achieving goals—that is very different than how we have been educated and raised. It is an approach which lends itself to the natural emergence of psychic experience.

Our modern Western culture offers many benefits but also comes with intense pressure. Constant demands are placed on our time and attention which usually take precedence—so our natural inclinations and spontaneity are pushed to the back burner time and time again. We tend to value and reward strictly rational approaches with tangible results as opposed to fluid, spontaneous experience and creativity. Seth's "magical approach" involves the natural person and their experience of reality in a free, non-programmed way. To flow and allow one's complete presence and involvement in the moment, which gives way to the next moment inviting further curiosity, inspiration, and discovery. To be spontaneous is to be fully engaged in your own unique experience of time and your actions within it. In Seth's magical approach, exercising one's natural psychic abilities becomes less a process of seeking data and information in a strictly linear, rational manner, and more a flow of curiosity and conscious engagement in the present moment. The answers emerge naturally through direct experience and not as a rational data input.

But we may be divided from ourselves in ways that bury our natural gifts including intuitive insights—what we would call psychic experiences. This is because we are dissociated from ourselves within the experience of our pressured day and are conditioned to place our attention outside ourselves completely. Yet our psychic perceptions are a natural part of the overall functioning of our wide-ranging consciousness though not perceived as such in our very time-pressured society.

Jane Roberts reflects on the concept of "magic" and the spontaneous occurrence of "magical" psychic events. She comments, "We were immersed in 'magic' no matter what we called it, that manifestation of telepathy and so forth, were just places where our magic 'showed'" (Roberts, *Magical Approach* xix). Seth's "magical approach" calls us to experience our lives, indeed the moments each day, with a completely different orientation: one involving a totality of experience and a more natural way of relating to time. In this framework, our psychic or seemingly "magical" experiences emerge spontaneously as a part of the overall experience, rather than being sought in a more linear, rational way and viewed as a distinctly separate and unusual experience. This would be conducive to more psychic experiences as a matter of course. How can we shift our orientation into this spontaneous flow in a way that also accommodates our busy lives?

Many of us have jobs, families, responsibilities and can often feel quite pressured and not the least bit spontaneous. If we work full time and have our arms full of responsibilities, we may over-schedule our days and divide up the hours and moments of each day in a very structured way. We may charge from one planned activity to the next, and never truly immerse ourselves in the whole experience, participating in a way that fulfills us. Seth talks about what he calls "assembly line time" where there is a culturally imposed sense of time and how to best "spend it." It is different than natural time which follows the earth's rhythm, the seasons, the moon's cycles and tides, the light of day and the dark of night. It is cultural time which overlays natural time by imposing calendars, clocks and hours that drive our collective activities—our timely arrival at meetings and our deadlines. Obviously, cultural time is valuable because it enables us to coordinate our activities and timeframes collectively, and so that we can reach our goals and complete our projects in agreed upon ways. But it can also rob us of our natural enjoyment of the moments of our day and our freedom to experience them in the ways we choose. Seth says, "The main point is indeed the importance of accepting a different kind of overall orientation – one that is indeed not any secondary adjunct, but a basic part of human nature...All of this involves relating to reality in a more natural, and therefore magical, fashion" (Roberts, *Magical Approach* 2). To return to our own playful and spontaneous nature means pushing back on certain elements of our lives that pressure us into "assembly line time."

To provide for ourselves financially, we can feel a great deal of pressure to "use time" to earn money and produce what we need to survive. We may also be conditioned to value only "productive time"—spending time only in the achievement of tangible goals. And if we simply use the moments of our day freely, we are wasting time and should feel guilty. This can keep us entranced in the culturally imposed "assembly-line time" and feel there really is no choice or alternative way of moving through our lives.

> The assembly-line time and the beliefs that go along with it have given you many benefits as a society, but it should not be forgotten that the entire framework was initially set up to cut down on impulses, creative thought, or any other activities that would lead to anything but the mindless repetition of one act after another.
>
> In other words, that entire framework is meant to give you a standardized, mass-produced version of reality (Roberts, *Magical Approach* 7).

Choosing to let go, allowing more and more of our day to flow, may seem impossible or even trigger fear. We may feel we are being irresponsible or will forget our obligations and begin to fail in the world. Or we may have unconscious fears of our wilder, less controlled nature and feel it is dangerous. We then block our efforts to surrender to our spontaneous nature.

> Many people, however, fear spontaneity; it evokes extravagance, excesses, and dangerous freedoms. Even people who are not so fervently opposed to spontaneity often feel that it is somehow suspect, distasteful, perhaps leading to humiliating actions. Spontaneity, however, represents the spirit of life itself, and it is the basis for the will to live, and for those impulses that stimulate action, motion, and discovery.
>
> In the truest regard, your life is provided for you by these spontaneous processes (Roberts, *Way Toward Health* 251).

I have been active in the Seth Online Study Group with the Seth Center for many years now. About five years ago, I remember our group was focused on spontaneity and learning to let go more and more into this natural orientation. I remember struggling with my own permission to let go and follow my spontaneous nature—to allow my days more natural flow and flexibility. An important aspect of Rick Stack's online study group is dream work: remembering and recording dreams and listening to the messages offered through this aspect of our psyche. During this period of time, I had dozens upon dozens of dreams about prison. I was usually a prisoner, but sometimes I was the jailer. They would be different prisons with different things happening and some of them were even funny. These dreams kept on coming and I couldn't find the keys to release myself. Finally, about a year later, I had a lucid dream in which I awakened with my full conscious faculties in the dream, and realized I was experiencing a dream. I was in a prison yard walking around and there was a little girl with me, maybe seven years old. We were watching a very lively street fair happening along the road outside the prison fence—it looked like great fun on this beautiful summer day. When I realized I had control over the dream environment, I materialized a bolt cutter and decided to cut the chain link fence open so I could free myself. The little girl asked me if she could come with me, and I said, "Yes, but promise me you won't run out into the street." She agreed and I cut the fence open, liberating us both. She looked at me and smiled and ran right into the street and disappeared into the fair. When I awakened, I was ecstatic—I'd finally freed myself from prison. At first, I wondered why the girl ignored her promise to me not to run into the street. Then I realized the girl represented the *spontaneous me* who needed to reject some rules and conditioning in order to be free and gain ownership of her life. I thought I had given her sage advice not to run into the street for her own safety. But it was a street fair and the traffic was blocked from this dreamscape! Her smile told me she had discerned what's safe for her and what is "just a rule." She broke my rule and joined the fair—obeying her own truth instead. After this very powerful lucid dream, I never dreamt about prison again.

I had the epiphany soon after that we must break some rules to free ourselves; we need to shed the conditioning that binds us. This sometimes feels counterintuitive—like we should feel guilty because we are breaking rules or becoming nonconformists. But the externally imposed rules may be the barrier standing between us and our freedom and knowing what's right for us. I encourage the rebel in you to examine the rules you live by moment to moment. Are they yours? Or do they just serve someone else or another system? Do you agree with them? Many rules are irrational or counterproductive and should be dispensed with. Which rules make sense to you given the circumstances of your life and your personal values?

Examine your thinking and what drives your behavior—which beliefs imprison you and block your spontaneity? Now, get out your bolt cutters! This is your life and only you can free your mind.

SOME SUGGESTIONS TO SUPPORT YOUR SPONTANEITY

Suggest to yourself that letting go and moving into your own natural flow is possible and indeed your natural orientation. You can begin by suggesting to yourself you will easily experience your spontaneity for at least a few minutes every day, with the goal of increasing it. You may have a pressured job and your boss is a maniac so choosing a time before or after work may be better to begin with. Take a few minutes to breathe and come back into your body and the present moment is a good start. Then maybe engage in an enjoyable activity that you know puts you in "your zone." Maybe dusting off that old painting you set aside and getting your easel back out, going for a run, writing some poetry, or going for a walk where you allow yourself to float in the "spacious present" and tune into your own unique experience of that moment. Ways in which you most easily let go can be varied so perhaps get out your psychic journal and begin writing about which activities help you to shift gears and experience your spontaneous nature. Journal about your own spontaneous nature and what you discover about yourself.

For me, I notice when I'm in my spontaneous flow there's a natural sense of appreciation for everything I am experiencing without wishing it would be something else. Acceptance and appreciation is a natural part of my own spontaneous experience. I stay out of effort and remain at ease because I'm not rejecting anything or trying to change and control things. I flow with it. Notice which emotions or qualities you experience when you're in the flow of your own spontaneous nature. Make a note of it with the intention of getting to know yourself better and raising your awareness of the qualities you experience in this particular state of mind. Validate your spontaneity and be playful.

145

Pushing back on extraneous obligations which consume your time is another important element of taking ownership of your life and the hours in your days. We may be programmed to feel that we must say yes to every request for help or volunteer ourselves for everything that cross-es our path. At the end of the day, many of the endeavors that consume our time may be unimportant to us and lack value. This can be a reflex-ive behavior so really examining what you say yes to and when it's best to say no, will help you take back ownership of your time. You may also review your calendar to see what regular commitments you devote time to and ask yourself if they still serve a valuable purpose. If not, consider releasing them from your schedule.

This is not to say you cannot experience your spontaneous nature at work or in other activities besides leisure and "free time." The goal is to eventually remain in a state of spontaneous flow while engaged in all aspects of your life so that your experience overall is fulfilling and a unique expression of your true self. But if you have resistance, as I did, when you approach this aspiration, finding those aspects of your day that are easier in which to shift gears—out of assembly-line time and into spontaneity—that's a good start.

I often used affirmations in this quest and return to them as need-ed. The following affirmations I adopted from the Seth Online Study Group, other students of the group, or I wrote myself. I share a few of them here with you. I encourage you to use those you like and to write some of your own as well.

- I relax and go with the flow of my being.
- I effortlessly take charge of my focus moment by moment.
- I find it easy to be spontaneous.
- I am the key to my freedom.
- I use time creatively and spontaneously.
- I am in the flow of the "magical approach."
- I move freely into the flow of my spontaneous nature.
- I unburden myself from tasks and obligations that lack value.
- I am happy, safe and free.

The "mindfulness" movement is similar in its intent to cultivate a presence in one's moment to moment experience and appreciation of time. If you have been practicing mindfulness in your life, it can provide a doorway to sustained experiences of your spontaneity. Mindfulness helps one to be fully aware of the body and its sensations, to disconnect from thoughts about the past and future and instead zero in on the "now." Thus, you'll stay fully and consciously engaged in each of your actions in the spacious present. I think of spontaneity as a natural outgrowth of mindfulness. To me, spontaneity is the expression of a person's unique style of moving through each moment to consciously co-create with life in its unfoldment. It is where our inner universe intersects with the outer universe, and we contribute our own unique action to the flow of life in a most personal way. Also, spontaneity is a very active approach fueled by curiosity. Our curiosity is the natural way we "ask ourselves" what we seek to know. We ignite creativity and magical events that then *attract those experiences which contain our answers.* The satisfaction we feel then fuels further discovery. Our extrasensory perceptions emerge as a natural part of the spontaneous process.

As my days became more spontaneous, I experienced some very expansive states of consciousness. I remember walking with my elderly mother in Alameda, CA on many afternoons. She progressed through years of dementia and so we couldn't converse with one another as we had in the past. So instead, we often walked quietly around the neighborhood and simply enjoyed our afternoons together. On three occasions, I spontaneously experienced what Seth calls, the spacious present. Suddenly without notice, it seemed all time stopped and my awareness expanded outward instantaneously. I dissolved into, and became a part of, the infinite present, where the moment has no beginning and no end. My whole being felt a profound appreciation for my mom, a moment with her never to be re-experienced and more precious than I can express. The quality of the light was surreal, and I knew I had awakened to my true self. Assembly-line time dissolved and the veil was lifted revealing my true nature and the breathtaking magnificence of our living universe. This was born of my spontaneous experience—moments shared with my mom on a few completely ordinary afternoons. My mother died a few years ago and I can still visit those moments in my mind and appreciate the vast wonder of our lives and the precious time we spend together on earth, never to be repeated.

I encourage you to cultivate your own spontaneity. To invite it back into your life like an old forgotten friend. See where it takes you. Enjoy the moments of your day and experience them in a way that is uniquely you. Cultivate your flow and learn how to validate yourself for spontaneous time rather shaming yourself for not "spending it productively." Seth says that spontaneity knows its own discipline. You may find you're actually more "productive" when you are in a state of increased flow and creativity. Living our lives fully and magically gives way to our natural heritage and full range of conscious experience, including psychic perceptions and a deeper appreciation of ourselves and our time here on this planet.

Chapter 11

Beloved

I am extremely fortunate to live such a blessed life with so many wondrous opportunities and experiences. I've had the honor of performing about 8,000 readings since I began my clairvoyant journey. Clients have come to me for a variety of reasons including blocks to fulfilling their aspirations and goals, challenging relationships, confusion around life purpose, career difficulties, and health problems to name a few. But I have to say, the most common problem is a struggle with loving themselves. I find so many pictures and thoughtforms revealing a client's basic mistake in understanding themselves and their intrinsic value. Many clients struggle with recognition of their own unique beauty and value and have rejected and turned away from themselves. At the root of their problems is loss of love for themselves—self-judgment, shame, loathing or rigid perfectionism—resulting in a longstanding, persistent state of self-alienation. Multiple tendencies and dysfunctional behavior patterns often overlay this problem and seem to be the cause of their unhappiness, but at the bottom of the stack of pictures is a lonely, abandoned person.

Self-abandonment often breeds patterns of thinking and behaviors that are counterproductive and deeply painful. Poor choices are made and precious time is wasted. I'm not a psychologist, and I'm sure there are many other causes of some of these patterns I've referred to, but spiritually speaking, the most common problem people have is an inability to see themselves, accept themselves, and love themselves. The person who can't let go of an infatuation with someone they hardly know, may really be desperately craving self-recognition and love. This need is projected out onto another person whom they believe must deliver this recognition, acceptance, and love. But underneath it all, the vacuum created by their own self-abandonment is driving their obsession.

Loss of self-love is very understandable given the programming we undergo throughout our lives which often invalidates our authentic nature and sometimes quirky ways of moving through the world. Subtle and not-so subtle pressure from family, social media, educational and religious institutions, and mass media messaging can smother and invalidate the best of us seeking to find our way in the world. Repetitive negative messaging from others, often early in life, creates a pressure to collapse into the false picture of self and wear that picture day in and day out even if it doesn't fit. Eventually we forget who we are and experience an amnesia we carry into adulthood. We may feel extremely angry and not know why; we may feel empty and directionless; or we may create work-arounds to help us fit in—that is, like excessive people-pleasing or other over-compensating behaviors.

The good news is we have complete authority in our lives as adults to reject these negative messages, to expel them from our energetic space— our field of consciousness—and reclaim our true nature. We are not victims who need to settle for this state of being for the duration of our lives. I believe that we choose the time we incarnate, our families, our circumstances and our prime life lessons before we arrive in each particular incarnation. This may be the challenge you need to arrive at self-love—to learn to fight for yourself and validate your own intrinsic value as the unique human only you know how to be.

I think the majority of us experience self-alienation in varying degrees and for different reasons. Making the choice to heal any and all pictures you harbor in your energetic space—any messaging that misrepresents you, your identity and your value—will restore your sense of self and empower your life. I'm here to cheer you on and provide you some tools to heal the old wounds that divide you from yourself.

Many sense resistance moving forward in this quest because it can be scary, because it will create change. Sometimes a terrible situation or condition feels safer because it is familiar. Acknowledging your own true self and returning to love is the most important work you can ever do. It is a person's greatest achievement. And in the spirit of Amelia Earhart's wise words: "Courage is the price life exacts for granting peace."

If you feel you are in a self-rejecting stance in life, I encourage you to journal about this and get your feelings out on paper. That can help you to begin to separate from it. Also, ask your dreaming self for suggestions about how best to move forward. I caution you not to go into victim mode. Empower yourself as an adult. You have the power to heal yourself and your life. In fact, you are the only person who can heal your life. As an adult, you are in full charge of your life force and the power to create change. Believe in that. Victim identities are self-defeating and I believe basically false. Instead, create affirmations reflecting your power and resilience as a spirit.

Below, is an exercise I often recommend to clients. It is creating a gratitude list—but a list of admirations you have for yourself on your own terms.

Exercise 16
Creating a Self-Gratitude List and Self-love Practices

*Get out your journal and begin to list all those characteristics, attributes, accomplishments, qualities, and actions you have taken during your life *that you appreciate about yourself.* The important thing is that they are *your sense of appreciation coming from your own perspective and values, not someone else's.* Your gratitudes may be big or small and can include absolutely anything you appreciate about yourself. Here are some examples to get you started:

"I love my smile and I'm grateful it's mine."
"I gathered the courage in 4th grade to join the spelling bee even though I was super scared. I'm grateful I'm the kind of person who can do things even when I'm afraid."
"I'm grateful for my silly sense of humor."
"I'm grateful I decided to finish college and get my degree when I really thought it was out of reach and I would fail."
"I'm really grateful that I'm a kind person. I took time to talk to that stranger yesterday even though I was in a rush. I could tell my kind words helped."

Every day sit down and write a few more gratitudes about yourself and keep the list going. When you finish writing for the day, stop and close your eyes and breathe in the gratitude you have for yourself. Feel it in your body and remember who you are. Validate yourself—defined by you alone and on your own terms.

*Next visualize a rose outside your aura and fill it with exactly what you need that day. Maybe you want levity and fun, maybe you need a hug, maybe you want to feel peace and calm. Decide what you need and send it over to the rose, see the rose absorb it all. See if the rose changes color, the vibration of those qualities you want to give to yourself.

*Now float the rose into your aura and over your crown chakra. Allow the energy and goodness in that rose to pour into your crown chakra and fill your entire body and energy field. Feel it soothe and nourish you. Take a few deep breaths as you receive this gift from yourself.

*Finish with an affirmation such as, "Love is all around me. I love myself fully and unconditionally." Find one that resonates with you that day and say it aloud. Thank yourself for this well deserved gift of self-love and validation.

Repeat this daily and keep your list of gratitudes handy. Celebrate who you are. This is the beginning of change, a return to yourself and an appreciation of your unique self and the contribution you make in the world just by being you.

This exercise, and all the others in this book, are practical ways you can reconnect with yourself and experience the magnificent range of consciousness that is your multidimensional self. You can free yourself from the confinement of old conditioning and pictures that limit your experience and dull your perceptions. My hope is that eventually enough people reclaim their natural psychic abilities so that clairvoyance, telepathy, remote viewing, psychokinesis, clairaudience, mediumship, precognition and all other forms of "magic" become so commonplace as to be considered "ho-hum." For such an advanced culture, it is high time.

Your soul calls you to stand taller than your fears. Pluck the pictures out of your energy field that tell you lies about yourself and drop them like garments to the ground. Tread on them. Be fierce in your sovereignty. Then shine your light brightly. Your light in this incarnation is the only light of its kind—it is unique on this earth and after you, will never shine in this particular way ever again. Know you are beloved.

"And did you get what
you wanted from this life, even so?
I did.
And what did you want?
To call myself beloved, to feel
myself beloved on the earth."
— "Late Fragment" by Raymond Carver
(Carver)

Conclusion

I hope in reading this book you have discovered some fascinating things about your own multi-dimensional nature and psychic abilities. Our energy system is wired for psychic functioning—it is a built-in function of our chakras. We simply need to rediscover these forgotten parts of ourselves, then validate and exercise them. For so long in our Western culture these abilities have been dismissed as false, fraudulent, impossible, delusional, or evil. With more and more people embarking on their own spiritual journeys and engaging in meditation and other spiritual practices that activate their higher chakras, these psychic experiences will blossom naturally of their own accord. These faculties are as real as our nose and toes and are ours to use freely and joyfully. It is our birthright to embody and experience the entire spectrum of our consciousness—not the narrow band in which we have been confined. As we free ourselves and embody our magical natures—the truth and power of who we are will be revealed and astonish us. It's only a matter of time before the "skeptical house of cards" folds and the truth about our natural psychic abilities becomes more widely acknowledged, accepted and applauded.

I encourage you to practice the exercises in this book patiently. Consider forming a small group of friends interested in doing this psychic development work together. This builds energy and enthusiasm that can fuel your exploration through mutual support. In the back of this book, I have included a number of resources. The Psychic Horizons Clairvoyant Training Program, the Seth Online Study Group, and many other programs are available to support you on your clairvoyant journey. I have also listed a myriad of outstanding books on this material which provide more information and direction in various forms of psychic functioning. Finally, I have included a list of some of my favorite affirmations. I encourage you to play with them and create some of your own.

Above all, it is my hope you will engage in an active dialogue with your inner self and learn to "ask yourself" for the answers and wisdom you thirst for. Through practice and through the cultivation of your spontaneous nature, a new expansive world of magic will unfold wherein you behold your spectacular personhood, your power as a conscious creator, and your clairvoyant vision. May it illuminate life's mysteries and unwind the challenges you face along your path.

I finish with an excerpt taken from Jane Robert's May 1972 ESP class recording. Seth was addressing students with the following powerful message:

> You are unique. There is no other in this or any universe like you. You are completely unique and through you the energy of All That Is flows in a completely unique, original, and never to be duplicated pattern. Therefore, what you are is eternally with meaning and with purpose and rings through the universe. ...The smile that you can give can be given in no other way...the touch of your hand can change a life in a way that no other individual could change that life... In each of you resides a uniqueness that is never really captured no matter how many times you are reincarnated. The self that you are now is unique and therefore it is highly important that you honor the self that you are through which the vitality of the universe shines. Honor your self as you would honor the gods then indeed do you also honor others. Deny your self and you deny others. ...So then, rejoice in what you are and each of you never to be duplicated, never again to be known, yet you are eternally forever renewed in mysteries that you cannot understand. So know your selves, honor your selves.[2]
>
> –Seth.

---

2 Excerpts taken from audio recording of Jane Roberts' ESP class held in May 1972 in Elmira, New York. Seth addresses students during the class, as channeled through Roberts. Recorded by Rick Stack, this excerpt is included with the permission of The Seth Center/New Awareness Network in Port Washington, NY.

Appendix

Holograms: You can create a hologram by sending a laser beam through an optical "beam splitter" in order to create two laser beams coming from the same source. The original beam, called a "reference beam," passes through a diffusing lens which expands its fine focus to a wide spreading, flashlight-like beam. *It has no contact with the object being photographed.* This beam is reflected by a mirror and onto a photographic plate.

The second beam, or "object beam" is used to illuminate the thing that is being photographed (Gerber uses an apple). This second beam bounces off the apple and meets the original reference beam and they "mix it up" so to speak, creating what's called an "interference pattern." *The photograph created from the interference pattern is a whole three-dimensional image of the apple even though the original reference beam landing on the photographic plate was never in direct contact with the object.* What is so fascinating about this is that "object beam" of light that interacted with the object being photographed *holds within it a three-dimensional record of the object itself.* " Holograms are energy interference patterns. Within this pattern, every piece contains the whole" (Gerber 47).

Diagram 4
Creating a Hologram

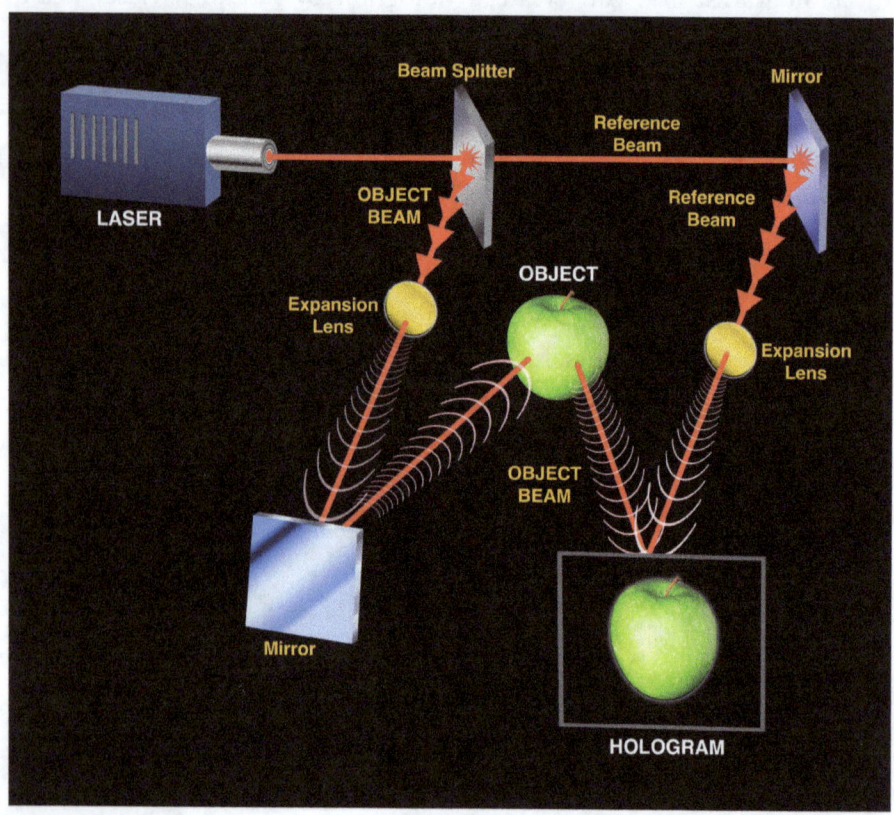

—Illustration by Ted Jalbert

Other Resources

Training Programs and Spiritual Development Resources

Psychic Horizons Clairvoyant Training Program/ Church of Natural Grace

PH is my favorite school of practical energy meditations and clairvoyant training. Their classes may be done remotely or inperson in San Francisco. 415-634-8800 www.psychichorizons. com email: psychic@psychichorizons.com

Pam Flowerday Intuitive Coaching

@PamFlowerday YouTube Channel launching in 2024 will offer psychic development videos with suggestions and guided exercises to support listeners in their continuing growth and healing.

Seth Center—New Awareness Network

The Seth Center offers all of Jane Roberts' books, Seth audio tapes, classes, intensives, conferences, and the Seth online study group and community. 516-869-9108 www.sethcenter.com email: sumari@sethcenter.com

Lynne McTaggart's Peace Intention Project and The Power of Eight

Get involved in group intention projects and help manifest a more peaceful world. Books, classes, retreats and upcoming intention projects can be found on her website: www.lynnemctaggart.com email: info@lynnemctaggart.com

Robert Waggoner Lucid Dreaming Resources

Find Waggoner's wonderful books on lucid dreaming as well as his workshops, online magazine, and dreams community at: www.lucidadvice.com

Institute of Noetic Science (IONS)

Dean Radin, Ph.D., is IONS chief scientist and author of *Supernormal: Science, Yoga, and the Evidence for Extraordinary Psychic Abilities,* as well as *Conscious Universe* and *Entangled Minds.* IONS mission is, "To reveal the interconnected nature of reality through scientific exploration and personal discovery." Workshops, webinars and conferences on human consciousness and the development of our human capacities are offered. www.noetic.org

Sacred Acoustics

High quality "brain entrainment" audio recordings with binaural and monaural beats designed to reduce the mind's chatter, help you relax more deeply, enhance presence, and reach expanded states of consciousness with greater ease. They also host spiritual development workshops and webinars. Check them out online: www.sacredacoustics.com

Recommended Books

Auerbach, Loyd. *Mind Over Matter: A Comprehensive Guide to Discovering Your Psychic Power*. New York, NY: Kensington Publishing Corp. 1996

Deloria Jr., The Vine. *Spirit & Reason*. Golden, Colorado: Fulcrum Publishing, 1999

Friedander, John & Hemsher, Gloria. *Basic Psychic Development: A User's Guide to Auras, Chakras & Clairvoyance*. SF, CA/ Newbury Port, MA: Weiser Books, 1999. Red Wheel/Weiser, LLC, 2012.

Gerber, Richard, MD. *Vibrational Medicine: The #1 Handbook of Subtle-Energy Therapies*. Rochester, VT: Bear & Company, 2001.

Huxley, Aldous. *The Doors of Perception & Heaven and Hell*. Harper & Brothers, 1954. Harper Perennial Modern Classics edition published 2009.

Martin, Annette. *Discovering Your Psychic World*. Campbell, CA: Artistic Visions, Inc., 1994.

Newton, Michael, Ph.D. *Journey of Souls: Case Studies of Life Between Lives*. Woodbury, MN: Llewellyn Publications, 1994.

Paramahansa, Yogananda. *Autobiography of a Yogi*. Los Angeles, CA: Self-Realization Fellowship, 1946, 1974, 1981, 1993.

McMoneagle, Joseph, *The Stargate Chronicles: Memoirs of a Psychic Spy*. Charlottesville, VA: Hampton Roads Publishing Company, 2002. Other recommended books by McMoneagle are *Mind Trek* and *Remote Viewing Secrets*.

McTaggart, Lynne. *The Field.* Great Britain: HarperCollins Publishers, 2001. New York, NY: HarpersCollins Publishers, 2008. Other recommended books By McTaggart are *The Bond* and *The Intention Experiment.*

Praagh, James Van. *Reaching to Heaven: A Spiritual Journey Through Life and Death.* A Dutton Book, Published by the Penguin Group, 1999. Also: *Adventures of the Soul—Journeys Through the Physical and Spiritual Dimensions.*

Radin, Dean, Ph.D. *Supernormal—Science, Yoga, and the Evidence for Extraordinary Psychic Abilities.* United States: Deepak Chopra Books, an imprint of the Crown Publishing Group, a division of Random House, Inc. New York, 2013,

Roberts, Jane. *The Coming of Seth (How to Develop Your ESP Power).* New York: Frederick Fell Publishers, Inc. 1966, 1974. Other books I have read by Jane Roberts are: *The Seth Material,* 1970; *Seth Speaks: The Eternal Validity of The Soul,* 1972; *The Nature of Personal Reality,* 1974; *The Unknown Reality: Volume 1,* 1977; *The Unknown Reality, Volume 2,* 1979; *The Nature of the Psyche: It's Human Expression,* 1979; *The Individual and the Nature of Mass Events,* 1981; *Dreams, "Evolution," & Value Fulfillment: Volume 1,* 1986; *Dreams "Evolution," & Value Fulfillment: Volume 2,* 1986; *The Magical Approach,* 1995; *The Way Toward Health,* 1997; *The Early Sessions, Volumes 19. The Personal Sessions* now also available. All Jane Roberts' books are available through The Seth Center at the website below. www.sethcenter.com email: sumari@ sethcenter.com

Roman, Sanaya & Packer, Duane. *Opening to Channel: How to Connect with Your Guide.* Tiburon, CA: HJ Kramer, Inc., 1987.

Stack, Rick. *Out of Body Adventures—30 Days to the Most Exciting Experience Of Your Life.* Chicago, IL: Contemporary Books, 1988. New York: Frederick Fell Publishers, Inc. 1966, 1974.

Stapely, Louise. *The Power of Affirmations & the Secret to Their Success.* Published by Louise Stapely in 2014.

Sui, Master Choa Kok. *Miracles Through Pranic Healing.* Manila, Philippines: Institute for Inner Studies, 1998.

Waggoner, Robert. *Lucid Dreaming: Gateway to the Inner Self.* Needham, MA: Moment Point Press, 2009. Another great book by Waggoner (with Caroline McCready) is *Lucid Dreaming, Plain and Simple: Tips and Techniques for Insight, Creativity and Personal Growth.*

Some Favorite Affirmations

I trust in my body's ability to heal itself every moment of every day. I enjoy spectacular good health and vitality now and always.

I am cancer free and enjoy exuberant good health.

My home is my sanctuary and I rest peacefully in its rooms.

I send healing love to all the cells of my body.

Every day in every way I am healthier and healthier.

I release all addiction energy now. I am filled with my own spiritual essence and thrive in every dimension of my being.

I feel a divine sense of self-worth and choose to see myself in a positive light.

I am a loving, strong and courageous person.

Love is flowing to me and through me at all times.

I love and accept myself and enjoy being me.

I love the person I am becoming more and more every day.

I release all invalidation and self-judgment from my life.

I am filled with unconditional love for myself.

I release depression from my life. Joy is my birthright and I experience it now.

I appreciate my creative energy and exuberant nature.

I am worthy of being loved and cared for tenderly and completely.

I naturally attract positive new friendships into my life.

I attract only healthy, loving and loyal people into my life. My relationships thrive.

I trust in the process of my life.

I move freely into the spontaneous flow of my life.

I am the key to my freedom.

I am in the flow of my life and attain my goals with ease and perfect timing.

I release the abuse and control of others from my life and step into my personal power now.

I honor my strength and resilience. I am the master of my destiny.

I release all guilt and confusion I have about wealth and abundance.

I trust myself to use my ever growing resources honorably and wisely.

I am now attracting the perfect career to match my talents.

I deserve to have a successful and fulfilling career.

I release all family trauma around money and am free to prosper now.

All the resources I need in my life manifest with ease and perfect timing.

I am creating a positive future for myself now.

Ask Yourself.

I am at peace with my past and trust in the process of my life.

Success is my birthright and I manifest it now.

I am divinely guided every moment of every day.

I am confident in my ability to create a positive future for myself.

I live in a safe universe.

My family and home are safe. I feel peaceful and secure.

I choose to feel safe and secure.

My confidence grows with each passing day.

I express myself clearly and confidently.

I believe in myself. I am my own best friend.

I am always connected to my highest good.

I trust myself to make the right choices in life.

I invite fun and laughter into my life.

I open my heart to the gifts of the universe.

I let go and trust the universe.

All is well in my world.

I invite magic and miracles into my life each and every day.

I always expect the best and that is exactly what happens.

My life keeps getting better and better every day.

I trust in my intuition and follow my truth.

I value my natural psychic abilities and they grow stronger every day.

I rest in the protection of infinite love.

I am beloved on the earth.

Honoring My Mom's Life
Through Her Poetry

Selected Poems by Jean S. Prodger (1923–2017)

YOUR PATTERN

I lay my trivial cares before You.
As a child
I have put them in a row
Like shells.
Upon the endless beach, they are small,
Sea crushed.
A gentle wave swells over them
Sweeping and
Washing them away, not forgotten, but made part
Of Your pattern.

THE END OF THE YEAR

The crows condemn the bitter sky;
October spins a bronze cocoon.
In yellowed elm the wind does sigh
That sleep will seek me soon.

A silver sun embosses pewter sky
Where drifting leaves, and scattered birds are etched.
That gray November's silent cry
Engraves its scars on aching soul outstretched.

The snowflakes fill the rutted road
And spread their white on sagging gate.
December shrouds an empty barn, the cracks that showed.
For dreams and deeds not done, winter will not wait.

IN CELEBRATION OF THE WILL

As the early blooming pear tree
Answers the call of spring
Bearing first and innocently
The risk of winter's sting.

Like the Norseman surging in running tide
His rude craft challenging all,
The first, the distant swell to ride
Seeking star and unknown landfall.

Like the scout first down the rushing river,
Or up the mountain peak,
Like the astronaut clutching rocket's quiver
And first to step for mankind's giant leap.

So my first choice, wrought in Soul's strife,
Vanished bravely and alone
Down the currents of my life,
But upon it my whole life has grown.

GAIA'S LAMENT

I am Earth.

Pirhouetted I before my lordly star,
My tiny sister by my side,
Swinging to the chorus from afar,
Breathing warmth and light.

Scarves of blue were wrapped me round,
Pearly mists perfumed my way.
White my crown and glowing my gown
With green and brown in bright brocade.

Now slowed and spent,
Barren and ravaged to the end,
My crown is smudge, my gown is rent.
Lost is my song in darkness deepened.

And yet,

I bore you, Other Life, as my best.
When you seek to leave my dying shell,
Remember the beauty of my living breast
And remember I loved Thee all too well.

REFLECTION

A spider makes his way across the walnut bar
Worn smooth by hands gone cold decades ago.
The minute, and short lived is
Intersecting the enduring past,
And time curls back on itself
like the ancient serpent of knowledge.
Remembering that time is nothing more than mind aware
And life is but a dream.

RETURN

Return, oh my soul, to your rest
In the desert night.
Hushed beneath the tent of
A thousand stars.
Take your rest, oh my soul.

Works Cited

Auerbach, Loyd. *Mind Over Matter: A Comprehensive Guide to Discovering your Psychic Powers*. New York: Kensington Publishing Corp, 1996. Print.

Cameron, Ron. *The Other Gospels*. Ed. Ron Cameron. Louisville and London: Westminster John Knox Press, 1982. Print.

Carver, Raymond. *Late Fragment*. New York: Grove Atlantic, 1989. Print.

Deloria Jr., Vine. *Spirit & Reason: The Vine Deloria, Jr., Reader*. Golden, CO: Fulcrum Publishing, 1999. Print.

Fitzgerald, Sunny. "The Secret to Mindful Travel? A Walk in the Woods." 18 October 2019. *Nationalgeographic.com*. Web page. 14 August 2022.

Friedlander, Hemsher. *Basic Psychic Development. A User's Guide to Auras, Chakras & Clairvoyance*. San Francisco: Red Wheel/ Weiser, LLC, 1999, 2012. Print.

Gerber, Richard M.D. *Vibrational Medicine: The #1 Handbook of Subtle-Energy Therapies*. Rochester, Vermont: Bear & Company, 2001. Print.

Huxley, Aldous. *The Doors of Perception*. New York: Harper Perennial Modern Classics. Reprint 2009, 1954. Reprint 2009. Print.

McTaggart, Lynne. *Results of the American Peace Intention Experiment*. 18 May 2018. Online web page. 17 August 2022. <https://lynnemctaggart.com/ the-results-of-the-american-peace-intention-experiment/>.

—. *The Bond: How to Fix Your Falling-Down World*. New York: Free Press, 2011. Print.

Radin, Dean PhD. *Supernormal: Science, Yoga, and the Evidence for Extraordinary Psychic Abilities*. New York: Deepak Chopra Books (An imprint of the Crown Publishing Group, Division of Random House), 2013. Print.

Roberts, Jane. "Seth excerpts." *Seth Excerpts from Roberts' ESP Class Recordings*. New York: Seth Center/New Awareness Network, May 1972. Audio recordings.

—. *Seth Speaks*. San Rafael: Amber-Allen Publishing and New World Library, 1972. Reprint 1994. Print.

—. *The Magical Approach*. San Rafael: Amber-Allen Publishing and New World Library, 1995. Print.

—. *The Nature of Personal Reality*. San Rafael, CA: Amber-Allen Publishing and New World Library. Reprint 1994, 1974. Reprint 1994. Print.

—. *The Unknown Reality, Volume 2*. San Rafael, CA: Amber-Allen Publishing and New World Library. 1997, 1979. Reprint 1997. Print.

—. *The Way Toward Health*. San Rafael CA: Amber-Allen Publishing, 1997. Print.

Sui, Choa Kok. *Miracles Through Pranic Healing*. Manila, Philippines: Institute for Inner Studies, 1998. Print.

Permissions

Thanks to Grove Atlantic for permission to use Raymond Carver's poem "Late Fragment." From *A New Path to the Waterfall* copyright ©1989 by the Estate of Raymond Carver. Used by permission of Grove/Atlantic, Inc. Any third-party use of this material, outside of this publication, is prohibited.

Thanks also to the Wylie Agency for granting permission to use "Late Fragment" in electronic versions of *Ask Yourself*. "Late Fragment" by Raymond Carver, Copyright ©1988 by Raymond Carver, 1989, 2000 by Tess Gallagher. Used by permission of the Wylie Agency, LLC.

Special thanks to Rick Stack, Director of the Seth Center, for permission to include two excerpts from audio tape recordings of Seth as channeled by Jane Roberts in the 1970s. Audio tapes of Seth may be purchased from the Seth Center/New Awareness Network, Inc. located in Port Washington NY. www.sethcenter.com

Many thanks to Inner Traditions and Bear & Company for permission to include extensive quotes from Richard Gerber's *Vibrational Medicine*. Their prompt reply to my request was greatly appreciated. *Vibrational Medicine* by Richard Gerber, M.D. published by Inner Traditional International and Bear & Company, ©2001. All rights reserved. http://www.Innertraditions.com Reprinted with permission of publisher.

Thanks to Fulcrum Publishing for permission to quote extensively from Vine Deloria, Jr.'s *Spirit and Reason* and for expediting this permission personally when the electronic permissions system failed. Permission granted for excerpts from *Spirit & Reason* by Vine Deloria, Jr. Published by Fulcrum Publishing, copyright ©1999. All rights reserved.

I acknowledge the meticulous research and writing of Dean Radin, PhD. His serious and yet playful book *Supernormal: Science, Yoga, and the Evidence for Extraordinary Psychic Abilities* provided exceptional material for Chapter Four of *Ask Yourself*. My excerpts fall within "fair use" and so permission was not requested, but my gratitude is wholeheartedly acknowledged. I applaud Radin's enthusiastic voice in the world of psychic phenomena.

Thanks to Amber-Allen Publishing & New World Library and New Awareness Network for continuing to make the Seth material available to readers around the world. I quoted from several of Jane Roberts' books and appreciate the use of this rich material. I am deeply grateful for Seth's wisdom which illuminated key concepts in *Ask Yourself* and appreciate the tireless work of these publishers to keep Seth's words alive.

About The Author

Rev. Pam Flowerday has performed 8,000 clairvoyant readings for people around the globe since 2001 and practiced Usui Reiki as a master practitioner since 1999. She was ordained by the Church of Natural Grace (Psychic Horizons) in 2019 after 15 consecutive years working as a spiritual counselor in Northern California. Pam has taught basic psychic skills courses in Alameda, CA and continues to coach people in the development of their clairvoyance. A graduate of University of California Santa Cruz with a degree in Environmental Studies in 1983, Pam worked in nature conservation until 1998 and still advocates passionately for the earth and environmental causes. She lives with her husband, Mark, and two dachshunds in Spokane, Washington.

Please Take a Moment to Post a Review

Reader reviews make a big difference to a book's success. I hope my book was enjoyable to read and helpful to you on your psychic journey. I would be grateful if you would take a moment to post a brief review on Amazon, Barnes & Noble, Goodreads, or the online bookseller from which you purchased your copy of *Ask Yourself*. Thank you!

www.ingramcontent.com/pod-product-compliance
Lightning Source LLC
Chambersburg PA
CBHW070703130626
46553CB00005B/1818